Old Social Movements?

Socialist History 25

Rivers Oram Press
London, Sydney and Chicago

Editorial Board

Stefan Berger
John Callaghan
Andy Croft
Allison Drew

Elizabeth Fidlon
David Howell
Neville Kirk
David Parker

Willie Thompson
Mike Waite

Editorial Advisers: Noreen Branson†, Eric Hobsbawm, Monty Johnstone, Victor Kiernan, David Marquand, Ben Pimlott†, Pat Thane

Editorial Enquiries: Kevin Morgan, Department of Government, University of Manchester M13 9PL or kevin.morgan@man.ac.uk.

Reviews Enquiries: John Callaghan, School of Humanities, Languages and Social Sciences, University of Wolverhampton, Wulfruna Street, Wolverhampton WV1 1PB or j.callaghan@wlv.ac.uk

Socialist History 25 was edited by Julie Johnson, Francis King, Kevin Morgan, John Callaghan

Published in 2004
by Rivers Oram Press, an imprint of Rivers Oram Publishers Ltd
144 Hemingford Road, London, N1 1DE

Distributed in the USA by
Independent Publishers Group, Franklin Street, Chicago, IL 60610
Distributed in Australia and New Zealand by
UNIReps, University of New South Wales, Sydney, NSW 2052

Set in Garamond by NJ Design
and printed in Great Britain by T.J. International Ltd, Padstow

This edition copyright © 2004 Socialist History Society
The articles are copyright © 2004 Meg Allen, Paul Burnham, Charles Hobday, David Young

No part of this journal may be produced in any form, except for the quotation of brief passages in criticism, without the written permission of the publishers. The right of the contributors to be identified as the authors has been asserted by them in accordance with the Copyright, Designs and Patents Act 1988

British Library Cataloguing in Publication Data
A catalogue record for this publication is available from the British Library
ISBN 1 85489 158 8 (pb)
ISSN 0969 4331

Contents

Notes on Contributors v

Editorial vii

'Weapons of the Weak' 1
Humour and consciousness in the narratives of members
of Women Against Pit Closures
Meg Allen

The Squatters of 1946 20
A local study in national context
Paul Burnham

Agency and Ethnicity 46
A pamphlet by the East London (Jewish) Branch
of the Social Democratic Federation
David Young

Edward Terrill and the Fifth Monarchy 61
Charles Hobday

Forum 80

Reviews 88

Books to be remembered (8)

Thomas Hodgkin, *Letters from Palestine, 1932–6* (John Saville)

Catherine Hall, Keith McClelland and Jane Rendall, *Defining the Victorian Nation: Class, Race, Gender and the British Reform Act of 1867* (David Goodway)

John Shepherd, *George Lansbury: At the Heart of Old Labour* (Matthew Worley)

Ahmad Alawad Sikainga, *'City of Steel and Fire': A Social History of Atbara, Sudan's Railway Town, 1906–1984* (Hakim Adi)

Vladimir Mau and Irina Starodubrovskaya, *The Challenge of Revolution: Contemporary Russia in Historical Perspective* (Monty Johnstone)

Bob Jessop, *The Future of the Capitalist State* (John Callaghan)

Andy Croft, *Comrade Heart: A Life of Randall Swingler* (Jean Jones)

Matthew Worley, *Class against Class. The Communist Party in Britain Between the Wars* (Mike Squires)

Kevin Passmore (ed.), *Women, Gender and Fascism in Europe, 1919–45* (Roger Griffin)

Neville Kirk, *Comrades and Cousins: Globalization, Workers and Labour Movements in Britain, the USA and Australia from the 1880s to 1914* (John Benson)

Andrew Taylor, *The NUM and British Politics, Volume I: 1944–68* (Keith Gildart)

Bryan D. Palmer, *Cultures of Darkness: Night Travels in the Histories of Transgression* (Neville Kirk)

Notes on Contributors

Meg Allen works at the University of Salford. Her PhD (Manchester, 2001) was on the community-based politics of Women Against Pit Closures.

Paul Burnham has been a tenant activist in Wycombe and Haringey and is presently a postgraduate student at Birkbeck College.

David Young's PhD (Durham, 2003) was 'People, Place, and Party—the Social Democratic Federation 1884–1911'. He now teaches history and politics in the UAE.

Charles Hobday is a poet and biographer. His study of Edgell Rickword, *Edgell Rickword: A Poet at War*, was published by Carcanet Press in 1989.

Socialist History Titles

Requests for back issues to ro@riversoram.demon.co.uk

Previous issues of *Socialist History* include:

14 The Future of History
...roundtable discussion with Jim Sharpe, Peter Jones, Mike Savage, Eileen Yeo, Kevin Morgan and Richard Evans...
1 85489 109 X

15 Visions of the Future
...David Purdy on utopian thought; Philip Coupland on utopia in British political culture; Maureen Speller on the future in science fiction...
1 85489 115 4

16 America and the Left
...David Howell on syndicalism; Neville Kirk on American exceptionalism; Kevin Morgan on the British left and America...
1 85489 117 0

17 International Labour History
...Sheila Rowbotham on working class women's narratives; Karen Hunt on internationalism and socialist women; Paul Kelemen on Labour's Africa...
1 85489 119 7

18 Cultures and Politics
...Matthew Worley on the Third Period; Andrew Whitehead on Red London; Martin Wasserman on Kafka as industrial reformer...
1 85489 123 5

19 Life Histories
...Richard Pankhurst on Sylvia Pankhurst; Andy Croft on Randall Swingler; Malcolm Chase interviews John Saville on the *DLB*...
1 85489 129 4

20 Contested Legacies
...Mark Bevir on socialism and the state; Matt Perry on the Hunger Marches; David Renton and Martin Durham debate gender and fascism...
1 85489 135 9

21 Red Lives
...Till Kössler on West German communists; Margreet Schrevel on a Dutch communist children's club; Tauno Saarela on characters in Finnish communist magazines...
1 85489 141 3

22 Revolutions and Revolutionaries
...John Newsinger on Irish Labour; Allison Drew on experiences of the gulag; Edward Acton, Monty Johnstone, Boris Kagarlitsky, Francis King and Hillel Ticktin on the significance of 1917...
1 85489 141 3

23 Migrants and Minorities
...Shivdeep Grewal on racial politics of the National Front, Keith Copley and Cronain O'Kelly on the British Irish in Chartist times; Stephen Hipkin on rural conflict in early modern Britain...
1 85489 155 3

24 Interesting Times?
...David Howell interviews Eric Hobsbawm; John Callaghan on reviews of *Interesting Times*; Ann Hughes on Christopher Hill's work; Cambridge communists reminisce...
1 85489 157 X

Editorial

How often in contemporary discussions of the left do we hear of how 'post-1968' the politics of class and the labour movement has given way to new social movements based on gender, ethnicity, sexuality, consumer as well as producer interests, and a whole host of other forms of identity? In this issue of *Socialist History*, our main features show, not so much how deep the roots of the new social movements really are, but how the politics of labour movements were always more diverse and contested than is often suggested.

Chronologically, Meg Allen's article on Women Against Pit Closures is the most recent in its subject-matter, but at the same time deals with one of the core constituencies of traditional labour history in the shape of the miners. Often coalfield history was impervious to issues of gender and the sexual division of labour on which the masculine institutions of mining communities were based. If the work of historians like Angela John did much to change this picture, so too did the central role which women played in defending their communities in the miners' strike of 1984–5. Drawing on the insights of oral historians like Allessandro Portelli and Luisa Passerini, Meg Allen uses interviews with women active in the strike to show how the narratives they constructed, and even their very omissions and hesitations, illuminate how the women negotiated and to some extent subverted the hierarchies of the coalfield community.

Forty years earlier, the major social issue confronting post-war Britain was not so much industrial unrest as the shortage of housing. Though, not for the first time, homes fit for heroes were promised in the longer term, not everybody was prepared to wait. The squatters' movements which resulted have already been documented by Noreen Branson and James Hinton, but Paul Burnham's is probably the most comprehensive local study yet published of the movement. Again using oral sources, as well as a painstaking survey of local archives and newspapers, his vivid account reveals a more militant aspect to the popular politics of the 1940s than has been recognised in several of the more recent accounts.

Another forty years back, at least in the East End of London, and the perennial problems of overcrowding and exploitation were to some extent overshadowed by an anti-aliens agitation stoked up by the yellow press. If that suggests contemporary parallels, so does the ambivalent reaction of some sections of the left. The Social Democratic Federation has come under particularly close scrutiny in this respect, but David Young in his contribution confirms once again that the SDF in reality was a far more complex and variegated organisation than used at one time to be assumed. In particular, Young examines a Yiddish-language pamphlet issued by the federation's East London (Jewish) branch to give an idea of the range of different perspectives and priorities coexisting within the same movement. It can usefully be read alongside our earlier contribution by David Burke and Fred Lindop on Theodore Rothstein and the origins of British communism (*Socialist History* 15).

Finally, in our last major feature in this issue, the poet and biographer Charles Hobday takes us well back beyond the origins of the labour movement to recover the millenarian ideas of Edward Terrill and the 'Fifth Monarchy' in late seventeenth-century England. As well as a fascinating piece of scholarship in its own right, the article also reminds us of how important these radical lineages have been for the twentieth-century left, and in this respect can be linked with the writings of Christopher Hill discussed in our last issue, and earlier contributions to this journal by Brian Manning. We are always keen to include contributions on earlier periods of history, and following Stephen Hipkin's article in *Socialist History* 23 hope that this can become a regular feature.

We are very sorry to note the deaths of two of our most valued editorial advisers: Noreen Branson and Ben Pimlott. Appreciations have appeared in the Socialist History Society *Newsletter*.

'Weapons of the Weak'
Humour and consciousness in the narratives of members of Women Against Pit Closures

Meg Allen

Story and narrative are the stuff of oral history. Throughout our lives we review our memories of events, pulling together the fragments and weaving them into a coherent narrative. Oral historians have sometimes focused on the narratives themselves, rather than how people choose to construct them, and this has been seen as a weakness in their method. How can reconstructed oral accounts give a true picture of historical events? The fallibility of memory means that the narrative is inevitably partial, people fill in the gaps through intelligent guesswork and elaborate the story for effect. In pasting over the cracks people can produce conflicting accounts of the same events, and their narratives appear so subjective and personal that it is hard to make any historical claims on the basis of them.

Yet the very weakness of oral accounts can also be their strength. On closer inspection an interested observer can begin to un-pick the construction of the narrative and identify the building blocks of the story. The way people decide to write their history, or painstakingly assemble their narrative, can be as revealing about a historical event as any hard fact gleaned from written records. Historians such as Allessandro Portelli have highlighted how the organisation of a narrative can reveal much about the relationship of the speaker to a particular event.[1] More than this, if we look more closely at oral accounts we often find elements which represent the presence of a collective viewpoint within an individual narrative. Approaching oral accounts in this way gives us access to the meaning, rather than the chronology, of historical events. This approach can be particularly useful when examining the history of a movement. By looking more closely at the things that activists choose to omit, or the points at which they stumble or become unsure, we can disclose points of friction or unresolved conflict in a movement. In highlighting common elements in different narratives we can also bring out the collective, yet unwritten, understandings that unite a movement.

Many oral historians have chosen to examine accounts in just this way, looking for omission and hesitation and unravelling the weave of the narrative. This approach has been most fruitful where the memory was painful or difficult to reconcile as in Passerini's research with workers in Turin, who had lived under fascism in Italy in the 1930s, or Thomson's work with Second World War veterans.[2] I will return to Passerini's work in my discussion, but first I use Women Against Pit Closures (WAPC) as a case study. I want to look at how women involved in the miners' support groups constructed a sense of themselves through collective narratives. The women shared a transforming experience during the strike, which was reflected in their accounts, yet they also shared a less obvious experience. They related a transforming experience of personal change and liberation, but they also struggled to express themselves at times. As women living in gendered mining communities their experience was complex and contradictory. Their narratives, and their consciousness of themselves, reflected this fractured experience.

The narrative of Women Against Pit Closures

Looking at oral accounts in this way, identifying points of discomfort, humour, or omission, became central to my research, which involved in-depth interviews with women who had been involved in the miners' strike of 1984–5. The research took place between 1998 and 2000, with women who had been active in Women Against Pit Closures. I looked at three areas, the North East, South Wales and the Yorkshire coalfields.[3] These discussions elicited many rich oral accounts of the change the women underwent as a result of their involvement in the dispute. These accounts were often 'triumphal', describing the amazing changes they had experienced in their understanding of the world. These were often well-rehearsed narratives, as the women had spoken at many meetings and on demonstrations and had been interviewed many times by journalists and researchers. Their accounts of personal change often had very similar elements and seemed to have changed little since the end of the dispute. In fact Joan Witham's 1986 autobiographical account encapsulates the sentiment that many of the women expressed in the late 1990s:

> I think my life had been one long lie. I am 50 years old now and I have been living in cloud cuckoo land. I am ashamed of my life because I taught my children lies. I told them the law was there to look after them, so they should not break laws. I told them we had freedom in this country.[4]

Witham vividly expresses the popular perception of this change in consciousness that was brought about by the strike. This is a narrative of consciousness raising that has been related many times in many different disputes. The common thread in these accounts is a 'road to Damascus' like revelation of the deep injustice in society. Many of the women of WAPC describe the scales falling from their eyes as they began to experience the prejudice of the government, the police and the judicial system. This change is recounted in the rash of autobiographical accounts that came out in the immediate aftermath of the dispute.[5] It was also reflected in the narratives of the women in my research.

There was no doubt that this change had been meaningful for the women. They described a profound revolution in their understanding of the social world that had been triggered by the strike. The women communicated the extent of the change through a series of anecdotes, describing their experiences and identifying certain points where they had been particularly struck by the inequity of the political system. These narratives were very moving and powerful and, even fifteen years later, the women often re-lived some of the emotions they experienced at the time. They were also very fluent when they described how their thinking had changed. These were narratives that were well rehearsed and forged during the dispute—in speeches and on demonstrations. The women had also tried to capture the change in the way they saw the world by writing poetry, songs and autobiography. These were emotive accounts of their experience, but they were also narratives that were produced for public consumption. They were the result of many discussions within the support groups and at conferences or on demonstrations. It is perhaps not surprising that the narratives had many common elements, constructed as they were in such a collective struggle.

These stories were not only central to the women's experience; they were also well documented both during and after the dispute.[6] Yet I also found that the women sometimes lost fluency when asked about the less obvious or more difficult aspects of their experience during the strike. They sometimes became hesitant when asked about conflict with men in their communities and found it hard to articulate the difficulties they had in establishing the women's groups. They also sometimes expressed contradictory opinions or beliefs about the strike and their role in it.

In these situations, humour was often used by the women to rescue the narrative. Humour was central to their narratives and the 'funny story' was used on many occasions to describe situations of conflict within the mining community. Historians have observed that when things are painful, difficult or hard to reconcile people struggle to find ways to incorporate them into a clear narrative.[7] They avoid certain subjects, they become inarticulate or they use humour to deflect lines of questioning. What the women stressed as important in their narratives were the changes they experienced in the way they saw the world. These were changes in consciousness, in their understanding of themselves in relation to the social world. Whilst their fluent narratives described the strike as a uniformly radicalising experience, their humour and hesitancy indicated points where this constructed story was interrupted. It was as if the triumphal story of 'a woman overcoming all odds to realise herself in struggle' was broken into by the realities of conflict within the community and difficulties in organising.

Despite their raised awareness, the women struggled to have a sense of themselves; the formation of their class consciousness seemed to be a complex and uneven process. There were hiccups in their narratives, as women struggled to be active in gendered mining communities and faced opposition from supposedly solidaristic comrades. These interruptions in their narratives were often identified by hesitancy, and humour was often used to bridge the gap between the ideal of solidarity between strike participants and the reality of conflict. These hiccups reflect the way in which the women's consciousness was constructed through pre-existing gender relationships. Simply in becoming active, women challenged the gender relationships of their communities. These interruptions led me to look more closely at the role of humour in mediating conflict in their communities and in reconciling interruptions in their narratives.

Community as mobilising force and gendered constraint

It is essential to have an understanding of the nature of the mining community to look at the experience of women in those communities. The women inhabited deeply gendered communities, which were also sustaining and solidaristic. Whilst women were totally integral to the continuance of the mining industry, they had no direct relationship to the pit or to the National Union of Mineworkers (NUM). Men and women tended to occupy separate spheres and since the men's sphere was that of the pit, the club and the union meeting, women were often excluded from public decision-making in their communities.[8] The women's relationship to the pit and the union, and so to public decision-making, was mediated through their husbands, father or brothers. The pit and the union, and the working men's club, were the public representations of class. These were places where the sense of being working-class was publicly defined. This meant that despite their very strong sense of class allegiance, the women occupied an ambivalent and marginalised position in their communities. Class was defined in the public sphere, whilst home, family and children were somehow separate and subordinate to that world.

At the same time women did have their own spheres of influence and drew on active support networks. Many of the women also experienced their communities as supportive and sustaining. One woman described how, during a period of illness, the other women of the village cared for her and her children on a rota basis.[9] The women inhabited a rich and supportive culture, one that often included many members of their extended family. The women appreciated the value of membership in their communities and saw feminism as a difficult position to hold in the context of their communities:

> I see myself as a feminist but I would distinguish that from what I call an 'ultra' feminist—that goes overboard. I have to live in a working-class area, I don't live in London, when I go to London I've associated with journalists and people that work in the City and all that sort of thing.[10]

Jean Stead describes this as the women being 'frightened of being called feminists or ending up like middle class women'.[11] To be an 'ultra' feminist meant they would have to leave their communities. Accepting some gender inequalities in their community seemed to be a trade-off for the benefits of membership. The women's narratives reflected this tension and also shaped the way they acted during the strike and made sense of their experiences.

Getting active—breaking gendered boundaries

In becoming politically active the women began to challenge the gendered behaviour which governed their communities. Their ambivalence about this challenge was apparent, not only because they felt uncomfortable about breaking the norms of their community, but also because in discussing the difficulties they encountered in the dispute they revealed their subordinate position in their communities. This ambivalence is revealed in their accounts of conflict with the NUM and men in their communities. They are often hesitant in these accounts and use humour to cover their embarrassment when they lost a battle with the local NUM or felt put down by men with whom they shared a picket line. Their stories reveal much about the organisation of gender in mining communities and the ambivalence and negotiation of women's position in those communities.

At the beginning of the strike the women's relationship to the NUM and to men in their communities was often clearly subordinate. Their role was to support the men and they often occupied positions in the kitchens or in food distribution which echoed their roles in the home. By that very work, however, they were thrown into contact with other women and forced into large-scale food preparation, ordering and distribution. Drawing on skills they had gained in the home they found that this 'women's work' could play a valuable role in the dispute and after the first few months of the strike women began to find confidence. Yet, their initial hesitation in taking on a public role was reflected in how they expressed their experience of the strike at the beginning. A woman from South Wales demonstrates this anxiety and uncertainty when she describes distributing sanitary towels to strikers and their wives:

> One occasion in the strike, this was hysterical, we went up fund raising to Devon…they said to us, 'What do we give you?' because we were getting loads of tins of corned beef, sometimes we were getting stuff that was stupid…but you do what you can…you know. At one meeting they asked anyway and one of the ladies said, 'The thing is we need things like soap, washing powder, sanitary towels!'. Well the next time we went up there they'd got boxes this big [arms wide] of sanitary towels which they proceed to give us! We are walking now through Devon with these boxes of sanitary towels and we were getting some very funny looks…Anyway when we got home we had to give these out, so we had lists of miners in the villages like…each week we had to give out food and clothing parcels and that, and sometimes we'd give out money, so we knew who was on strike like. Anyway this one day we went all around the village and we were knocking on the doors of the miners and giving a bag of tomatoes and a packet of sanitary towels, you should have seen the look on the faces of some of the men we gave them to! We said, 'Just don't ask, your wife will be glad of them!'[12]

The woman told the story with great humour, yet in telling it she was tentative and constantly checked to see if I, the interviewer, found the subject acceptable. Mining communities shared with the rest of society ideas of shame in association with menstruation, in distributing sanitary towels the women risked being the subject of ridicule. Yet at the same time there was exhilaration in the telling of the story. The strike provided a set of circumstances where they could break normal taboos and be open about menstruation because one of the women's everyday needs had become visible. It was a situation in which the women could break those taboos yet avoid the condemnation of men who might see them as feminists, who had abandoned a class allegiance which was central to the strike. In crossing those boundaries they challenged others in their communities. The humour in the story reflects this element of risk as they walked the tightrope between acting on issues that affected women, and losing their class allegiance.

In a similar way many of the women tell the story of their 'first speech'. Whilst many of them have gone on to be confident public speakers, their stories of their first speech reflect the lack of confidence they had at that stage. All the stories were peppered with humour and were often self-deprecating.

> Yes, the first place I went to was the AUEW [Amalgamated Union of Engineering Workers] in Birmingham, that wa' the first time, me and Maureen went and…err…it was a bit of a laugh really, we'd wrote notes on the train going down because neither of us had spoke and we'd sorted out…She said you speak first and I'll speak second…well we got to this upstairs room and it wa' like a big area meeting where there was loads of people round big tables…what the idea was that they was going to deal with their business first and at the end they'd ask us to speak, to put our case for donations…well of course we were so nervous we was both sat there smoking and the end dropped off of me fag onto the writing pad, me notes and it all went up in flames. Nobody said anything, so I'd lost me notes, Maureen didn't want to speak then…so I ended up just saying as it came and then Maureen did come back in after all…they took us for some food afterwards and they cracked up laughing, they said 'what it didn't do for us to hold us laughter in because we knew it were your first time and we didn't want to make you feel worse by laughing!'[13]

The woman went on to become a very proficient speaker, has since become a local councillor and now runs her own business with her husband. It is a very funny story, but the humour is self-effacing and belies her obvious competence. The women of WAPC were popular as speakers and this could sometimes cause conflict with NUM officials. In taking the role of speaker, as spokesperson for the dispute, many of the women moved out of their gendered and subordinate role and their self-deprecation expressed their uneasiness with this move. They were well aware of the criticism that they could attract when they took a leading role and tried at all costs to diffuse this potential. Solidarity was essential to the success of the strike and in taking a leading role women risked a conflict with the men which could threaten that solidarity. This awareness was constantly in their minds, the need to work collectively and to retain their position as mothers and wives in mining communities, whilst taking a role that contradicted that position.

Internal conflict was something that could have destroyed the dispute and it was essential to maintain solidarity and good relationships within their communities. The need for internal cohesion sometimes meant that women had to obey gendered rules. It was a tension they constantly negotiated in working with both individual men and the hierarchy of the NUM. As one woman said when asked if there was conflict with the local NUM or individual members:

> No we didn't really, not really…I mean there were a lot of meetings we didn't go to and I suppose there might have been a bit of that but we did what we wanted to do in the main, or what we felt necessary to do and we didn't have no major hassle with any of them, there was nothing…there was one chap, I got a little bit of grief off him, just once, I was annoyed at him…They [the women] got on with doing what they thought would give publicity and get things over to the public, and I think in all honesty so did the men but this was one on his own, this bloke got up my nose anyway! I wouldn't speak at one meeting because he was there, I said you are a male chauvinist pig and I've got no time for you [laughter]…That were in London…but…err…he were the only one I think…[14]

She found the experience of working alongside the men a largely positive one. Yet she clearly struggles to find ways to express the resistance and prejudice she found amongst a minority of men. In common with many of the women of WAPC she believed that all members of mining communities were also members of the working class and had the same interests. Yet this belief was difficult to reconcile with the prejudice they sometimes encountered. These kinds of hesitant responses were very much a part of the women finding their feet. A South Wales group member describes the first few weeks and months of the group:

> We decided that we'd form a miners' support group because it was happening everywhere you know! So we started to meet and we asked could we meet in the club in the big hall…but we were told we couldn't do that. There was a very strict chairman then and he'd grown up in there, but he said we couldn't do that unless we asked all the women in the village…like…erm…we made it for all the women in the village…and I think about twenty two women turned up. After time passed I suppose we were left with a core of about twelve…so err…we used to have differences with the men that was for sure…about going places, we couldn't go picketing particularly…err…instead of just getting up and going, we

should have just got up and gone...you know...but it was new for all of us so we just couldn't go, we were finding our feet...[15]

The hesitancy in her account says much about the early days of the dispute and how hard the women found it to have a voice in the strike. Again the women found themselves struggling to hold their role as wives and mothers in a very traditional community and play an active part in the dispute without undermining the community. As the dispute progressed the women began to hold this tension with more confidence. The strike inexorably drew them into more activity and their broadening experience made them more able to take on the union hierarchy and individual men in their communities.

'Brer Rabbit Fights Back'—humour as a weapon in the gender war

As the women became more active they came more and more into conflict with individual union members and with the NUM hierarchy. To negotiate these conflicts they increasingly used humour as to assert themselves, as a counter-attack to sexist attitudes and as a way to challenge restraints placed on their activities by the NUM. They could use jokes, or put-downs to dispute sexist behaviour, without directly contending for power.

There is little to guide the researcher trying to understand the role of humour in social and political resistance. Psychologists and anthropologists have struggled to understand the meaning of humour in human interaction. Within anthropology it is accepted that humour and jokes are often play a similar role in different cultures. Drawing on the work of Freud, Mary Douglas argues that as adults we learn to monitor our unacceptable unconscious thoughts. When we joke we relax this control and allow our hidden thoughts to show through. It is a situation where the unconscious is allowed to triumph. Douglas describes the joke:

> Since its form consists of a victorious tilting of uncontrol against control, it is an image of the levelling of hierarchy, the triumph of intimacy over formality, of unofficial values over official ones.[16]

In this sense humour is a weapon of the powerless, a way in which established power relations can be subverted without direct challenge. Women in the dispute found that humour could be used in this way, to challenge the men without being openly threatening. They were aware of their subordinate position and were keen to demonstrate that they did not accept that position passively but tried to challenge it whenever possible.

There is a fundamental paradox in the women's use of humour, in that their position as subordinate enabled them to mount this challenge. For a male NUM member to joke in a similar way within the union could be perceived as aggressive or contending for power. The women could use their gender, their supposed inexperience and their lack of power, to say things that would have been unacceptable from other supporters or strikers. In speaking out in this way they gained confidence and began to subvert the relationships in their communities:

> We'd have to promise before going in to the offices that we wouldn't say anything and that only one person was allowed to speak. Then I wanted to know one day, when Kim Howells was yak yak yakking, 'How come he gets to speak!' And they said he was the official note taker and I said 'oh Kim you've been promoted!'[17]

The women's position in relation to the NUM and men in the strike was complex and, at times, ambivalent. The women often acted under the direction of the NUM but refused to accept direct control by the union. As a result there was sometimes conflict between the women's groups and the NUM. The women would express these disagreements indirectly, by their behaviour on picket lines or in other actions during the dispute. In South Wales the ongoing conflict between the regional office and the women's groups surfaced over support for Arthur Scargill. The South Wales NUM hierarchy did not always agree with Scargill's style of leadership during the dispute, and as the strike progressed they sometimes expressed open disagreement with the Barnsley based leadership. Kim Howells even pointed out in February of 1985 that many South Wales miners wanted to return to work.[18] The women were staunchly behind the continuation of the strike and used their support of Scargill on this issue to taunt regional officials.

> I suppose they didn't hate us...but they didn't like us supporting Scargill, there was sort of like Scargill worship! We called ourselves 'Scargill's Angels' and we thought this was hysterical because we knew this was getting up everybody's noses, it was sort of like a pun on Charlies' Angels. We played it up something rotten![19]

Their support for Scargill had two functions; it expressed their political support for the continuation of the strike, and their opposition to any attempts by the regional office to control the women's groups. Again, it could be argued that such humour was a reflection of their weakness in the dispute, since Kim Howells and the regional officials in South Wales controlled resources and directed the strike locally. The regional office constantly attempted to direct the women's groups, who tried to maintain autonomy and attack the regional control whilst retaining a public image of solidarity. Yet, their use of humour as a more direct challenge illustrated the confidence the women were gaining in working together and in their opinions and the direction the dispute should take. At the same time this joking challenge enabled them to hold the increasing tension they experienced at being subordinate in a dispute where they felt their influence and activity to be increasingly important.

As the dispute progressed the sheer energy the women put into the struggle often meant they became increasingly pivotal in the local campaign. The women had a growing awareness of this importance, and the grudging acceptance of local NUM officials and members reinforced this sense of themselves. This was reflected in one woman's experience in the North East:

> The men just got sort of pushed to the sidelines, there was a big event at Christmas when all the turkeys came from abroad. Now I'd slept in that morning. I'd written all the instructions out as to what we were going to do and how we were going to plan this operation and everything, and I got a big thrill really because when I ran up, the NUM secretary was standing there with these instructions (laughter) and he was saying 'we canna start till Florence gets here!' Now really that was a thrill for me. Jacky was asking me and I thought 'eh this is fantastic', because it took a long time but we were working together at the finish, not at the start, and not three quarters through, but at the finish![20]

For women who were not as pivotal there were often small triumphs, experienced in the day-to-day work of the dispute. Slights, which would have been tolerated at the beginning of the dispute, began to be challenged. A woman from the North East was keen to stress how amazed she was by her own challenge to another 'chauvinist pig':

> The way some of them men down there used to act used to be bad. There was one man in particular used to just shove his cup down. We would be working or clearing up, and he used to come in and many a time he used to bring eight or ten cups back and he used to bang them down, stand there and he'd be like drumming his fingers like. And I just looked over

at him and he went, 'I want a cup of coffee'. Well I says, 'The coffee's there, and the urn's there' and he said, 'I'm not getting it, that's what you're down here for'. Well I just said, 'In your dreams pal! I'm not down here to feed you and if you want a cup of coffee you can go and get it or you can go away, because its bloody downright laziness.' I was flabbergasted I told a man off! I can't look at him to this day, I hate him ! Everybody was, like, looking like I'd lost it—but I stood up for myself![21]

This change came about not only by interaction with groups such as the NUM, but also by their bond as women. Through their work in largely women-only groups they began to gain a sense of their interests as women. This was something the women found difficult to put into words. They found the language of feminism to be alien; it did not fit their class circumstances and did not help them negotiate the tension they experienced as working class women in mining communities. The women's groups were a new experience of community, an experience that profoundly re-wrote their previous relationship with their families and communities. Women again expressed this experience of bonding, of women being together in a different kind of community, through humour and narrative.

Anthropologists have argued that humour is central to the development of community in the sense of informal and local groups. Mary Douglas uses a definition of community that is useful when talking about humour. She sees community as 'an undifferentiated field of friendship and acquaintance'.[22] As an anthropologist she deals with smaller scale interaction and sees the idea of community as inherently in opposition to the idea of structure and hierarchy. In these smaller groupings she argues that roles are defined by ambiguity and equality, and tend to be characterised by 'disorganisation' in terms of their loose structures and informal processes. In the formation of the women's groups we can see this localised 'disorganised' process at work, again often with humour as a facilitating element. Most importantly we can see that the bonding that occurred in the formation of the groups, and of a women's community, was central to the change in the women's sense of themselves and their belief in their ability to impact on their world.

Indicative of the development of this collective sense of themselves, was the willingness of the women to engage in activities as a group. In the early part of the strike they were invited on demonstrations or pickets, but later on they began to initiate activity. This is illustrated by one of the women from the Seaham group who remembers being in hospital during the dispute:

> I had a hysterectomy during the strike as well, I went for a smear and the doctor said he wanted to see me. Then the nurse came up and said the doctor wanted me in the hospital. Anyway the girls, aye it was a scream, they came up to Rywarp General Hospital with a banner and they took the buckets collecting along the way! They come in the ward with their banner and their buckets, I was sitting stiff, and I couldn't move with me stitches. But when they were collecting on the way up they were stopping the cars and getting money off the drivers.[23]

Although initially the women worked in single sex groups because they were not allowed a role in the local NUM campaign, the groups came to mean much more to them. Their strengths as women became very apparent in the groups and, as one woman from South Wales comments:

> I think it was different because we was women, because we used to have a good laugh, a bus full of women you know!…we was poor and everything but we used to enjoy ourselves, never do nothing wrong like. But I think if you are all women you lay yourself open more and enjoy yourself more than with your husbands, or whatever, and we really did, it was good![24]

This collective awareness of themselves was carried beyond the mining village. By the end of the dispute the women had been involved with sit-ins to get premises for their kitchens or had been arrested on picket lines. Women felt able not only to challenge the men in their own communities but were confident enough to challenge other groups, and even the press:

> Well I actually had a quote in one of the papers and somebody asked me what a feminist was and I said 'a woman with a brain!' [laughter]. It was the first thing that came into my head. I never went by the title of feminist but I always believed in women's rights![25]

The women's humour did not take the form of a standardised joke. Until very recently women have not appeared as formal comedians and it is usually men who inhabit the public world of humour. Women are often less likely to joke in mixed company than men and less likely to pass on a joke.[26] Women's' humour is more likely to be situational and revolve around everyday life than be around formal jokes. Humour was often the way in which they negotiated their ambivalence and made sense of the contradictions in their positioning their community. Mary Douglas argues that the role of the 'joker' is a position within the social world that is immune to 'comeback'.

From the stance of joker an individual may challenge with impunity the dominant social structure.[27]

In the majority of societies women's behaviour is monitored and is perceived as symbolically significant. Women's sexual behaviour is fenced, their moral virtue assessed and this social control is reflected in their freedom to joke or occupy the position of the 'joker'. This is borne out by the fact that women are often particularly absent from slapstick humour or horseplay. Communities are often defined in this way, by the behaviour of their members. The maintenance of a woman's reputation and her behaviour is often one of the cultural and gendered markers of community boundaries. In other words a community is *this* community because *our* women behave in a particular way. For the close-knit mining community, gendered behaviour was important. Gender defined roles, modes of behaviour and distinguished mining communities from other kinds of community. This constraint was reflected in the women's narratives through hesitancy and humour, but it also shaped their whole consciousness, their way of understanding and interacting with their world.

Oral history, gender and consciousness

The way the women used humour in their accounts of the strike revealed the deep tensions within gendered mining communities. The women's consciousness was formed in the context of subordination, but that subordination was challenged by their role as pro-active players in defence of the strike. The tension between their subordination, and their activity, meant that there was not always a clear relationship between their stated beliefs and what they actually did. They could be found expressing gendered beliefs about a woman's role in the home, whilst touring, speaking and picketing. Living in gendered mining communities meant that at times they had to express ideas that were out of step with their work in the dispute.

The purpose of my research was to look at the self-defined politics of WAPC and how the women constructed a collective identity through struggle. Since the idea of a radical change in consciousness was central to the women of WAPC, it was inevitably a central focus of my research. Yet contemporary explorations of the idea of consciousness seemed inadequate to the task of understanding the complex and interrupted narratives of the women I interviewed. I found that the tensions between action and belief amongst the women of WAPC stretched to breaking point existing models of consciousness. For example, both marxist and feminist models contained implicit assumptions about what constitutes a true class or feminist consciousness.[28] In this approach individuals are often measured against some sort of scale or typology that describes the essential elements of a 'radical consciousness'.[29] In comparison with such scales the women of WAPC were always found wanting.[30]

Models of consciousness also tended to regard it as something fixed, something that could be expressed in individual attitudes or opinions. Using this model, by recording people's opinions an observer can easily read-off, or assess their level of consciousness according to pre-set typologies.[31] Yet the women of WAPC often acted in ways which contradicted what they said. Their stated beliefs often lagged behind their actions. Women often appear as more reactionary in these assessments of consciousness, yet whilst they may not identify in the same way as men in terms of class, they can be more radical on other issues. Their lack of familiarity with established political systems can make them more open to different possibilities for action and more radical when they do act.[32] This was certainly true of the women of WAPC. This suggests a more complex reality in which women's beliefs and actions are shaped by their place in the world and the constraints on their action in it.[33]

In contrast to approaches that use opinion as a starting point, consciousness can be seen as something that develops as the actor responds to their situation.[34] It is not just about beliefs but the context and meaning behind the belief. Rick Fantasia in his work in a factory in the USA, spent time on the shop floor understanding the culture of the workplace and how group solidarity and consciousness was acted out in conflict.[35] Fantasia actually argues that the term consciousness has been too muddied for it to be a useful concept. He prefers instead to talk about 'cultures of solidarity', how consciousness is fostered and develops in collective interaction and opposition.

Fantasia is critical of the assumption that to act in the world, and to try to change it, someone should have a clear image of the world and a clear plan of action and change. He points out that there is a 'belief amongst academic observers that it is somehow necessary for men and women to encompass society intellectually before they can attempt to change it'.[36] Fantasia shares with many other commentators a profound unease with an analysis that misses out the role of lived and changing experience in creating consciousness. We can see this concern in the work of E. P. Thompson who argues for a more complex notion of consciousness, as contradictory and ambiguous.[37] Thompson examines the idea of 'custom', which he defines as people's common practices, and commonly accepted rights. He argues that this notion of custom could be used to resist imposition by employers or by the market. At the same time it was a resistance that called upon traditional forms and practices and could be conservative in its nature.

He makes the point that plebeian culture was rebellious, but often rebellious in defence of custom. This is a far more complex conception of consciousness and action—one that allows for tensions in belief systems and contradiction in radical action.

Historians have often been aware of the fluid dynamic between experience, consciousness and action. Luisa Passerini carried out research with workers in Turin, who had lived under fascism in Italy in the 1930s.[38] Her background research found that historical accounts tended to portray workers as spontaneously anti-fascist, yet there was also acquiescence to fascist rule in that period. Passerini was forced to question both her own assumptions and those of oral history. She found that she often received what she regarded as irrelevant or inconsistent answers to her questions, answers that most often took the form of jokes, anecdotes or simply silences. She could only explain these responses as a reflection of the pain and ambivalence of a generation that both detested the fascist regime yet found in it continuity with the past. Their silence and humour demonstrate shame in their complicity with the system. These interruptions in the narrative mark a 'scar' or a 'wound' in human experience. Their jokes show their irreverent resistance to the regime and anecdotes express the complexity of their time under fascism.

Passerini highlights the ways in which people can internalise their oppression, and how that internal ambivalence is expressed or shown through absences, anecdote, jokes and contradiction. Whilst the oral accounts are not factual representations of what happened they reveal much about the ambivalence the workers experienced under fascism: the experience of what Thompson called conservatism and rebellion. Whilst 1930s Italy and the miners' strike of 1984–5 in Britain are obviously very different contexts, there were similar silences and jokes which peppered the accounts of workers Turin in the 1930s and the women of WAPC in the 1990s. In both accounts humorous anecdotes and stories often illustrated points of conflict and difficulty. The women in my research used humour to bridge the gap between their conservatism as miners' wives and their rebellion as members of WAPC.

The work of Thompson and Passerini gives us a more profitable way of understanding consciousness. It is possible to trace a consciousness that is at once contradictory and ambivalent, formed out of praxis and shaped by relations of dominance and subordination. This approach helps us to understand more marginalised ways of seeing the world. For women, there is often no clear language to express their experience. Marjorie DeVault found this to be the case when she looked at women's experience of housework.[39] The women she interviewed often struggled to find the language and concepts to describe their everyday lives and work Their experience as housewives was marginal to the public world. There was no arena where women could discuss this aspect of their experience and so develop a common language and collective understandings. In this situation people struggle to speak and, as Sheila Rowbotham points out, 'borrowed concepts are like passed-down clothes: they fit badly and do not give confidence'.[40]

I wanted to look at the formation of the gendered class-consciousness of a particular group of women. By examining their oral accounts I found that the struggle to develop a marginalised, yet collective, consciousness involves at first hesitant and then more confident play with words and 'joking' challenge. In coming together the women were able to develop a collective sense of themselves and write a coherent 'story'. Yet this story was shot through with ambivalence, hesitancy and self-deprecation, features which reflected their ambivalent position in the communities. Their class-consciousness was, in turn, shaped by this ambivalent position and by their experiences of resistance during the dispute. In my research oral accounts were the key to understanding this unexpressed experience of ambivalence.

It was important to look beyond the tale at how the story itself was constructed. Using oral accounts in this way can open up new ways of understanding social action and can reveal points of conflict and the power dynamics of a social movement. It can also reveal alternative and marginal accounts of events. By looking at the account that exists at the margins of the 'triumphal' narrative we can begin to learn about the complex realities of knitting together a campaign. We can discover the process whereby certain accounts come to hold the legitimacy of truth. Most importantly we can begin to understand how different needs and interests are structured into a hierarchy in a campaign and how individuals negotiate those hierarchies.

Notes

1. Allessandro Portelli, 'The peculiarities of oral history', in *History Workshop Journal*, 12 (1981), pp.96–107.
2. Luisa Passerini, 'Work, ideology and working class attitudes to fascism' in Paul Thompson and Natasha Burchardt, *Our Common History* (London, 1982); Alistair Thomson, 'Anzac memories—putting popular memory theory into practice in Australia', *Oral History*, 18, 2 (1990), pp.25–31.
3. Meg Allen, 'Carrying on the strike: the politics of Women Against Pit Closures' (Manchester PhD, 2001).
4. Joan Witham, *Hearts and Minds* (London, 1986), p.100.
5. There are many autobiographical accounts of the strike; see for example Barnsley WAPC, *Barnsley Women Against Pit Closures*, (Todmorden, 1984) and *Barnsley Women Against Pit Closures Vol.2* (Todmorden, 1985); Eppleton Miners'

Wives Support Group, *Feelings Alive '84/85* (Hetton-Le-Hole, 1985); M. Jones, *Against all the Odds* (Sheffield, 1984); Chrys Salt and Jim Lazell, *Here We Go— Women's Memories of the 1984/5 Miners' Strike* (London, 1986); People of Thurcroft, *Thurcroft—A Village and the Miners' Strike* (Nottingham, 1986); North Yorkshire WAPC, *Strike 84/5* (Leeds, 1986); Worsborough Community Group, *The Heart and Soul of It* (Todmorden, 1985).

6. See Barnsley MWAG, *We Struggled to Laugh* (Barnsley, 1987); Lynn Beaton, *Shifting Horizons* (London, 1985); Coventry Miners Wives Support Group, *Mummy...What did you do in the strike?* (Coventry, 1986); Denise Fitzpatrick, Mary Cadwallader and Edith Armitage, *Ten Years on and Still Laughing* (Rotherham, 1994); Jackie Keating, *Counting the Cost* (Barnsley, 1992); Jill Miller, *You Can't Kill the Spirit* (London, 1986); Vicky Seddon, *The Cutting Edge—Women and the Pit Strike* (London, 1986).
7. Passerini, 'Work, ideology and working class attitudes to fascism'.
8. The women of WAPC were not initially allowed into NUM meetings and only the men made decisions about the strike and action. This was challenged over the course of the strike and women were, after a long battle, given associate membership of the NUM several years after the dispute.
9. Interview with Betty Cook, Tankersley, Yorkshire, 3 April 1998.
10. Interview with Jean Miller, Mapplewell, Yorkshire, 2 June 1998.
11. Jean Stead, *Never the Same Again* (London, 1987), p.307.
12. Interview with Kay Case, Treharris, South Wales, 13 March 1999.
13. Interview with Jackie Naylor, Mansfield, north Notts, 10 August 1998.
14. Interview with Jackie Naylor, 10 August 1998.
15. Interview with Hilary Rowlands, Markham, South Wales, 21 September 1998.
16. Mary Douglas, 'Jokes' in Chandra Mukerji and Michael Schudson, *Rethinking Popular Culture* (Oxford, 1991), p.297.
17. Interview with Sian James, Neath, South Wales, 4 March 1999.
18. See Bernard Crick, *Scargill and the Miners* (Middlesex, 1985), p.143.
19. Interview with Sian James, 4 March 1999.
20. Interview with Florence Anderson, Hetton-Le-Hole, Durham, 19 April 1999.
21. Interview with Jan Smith, Murton, North East, 12 April 1999.
22. Douglas, 'Jokes', p.307.
23. Interview with Margaret Nugent, Seaham, North East, 8 October 1998.
24. Interview with Pam King, Oakdale, South Wales, 11 March 1999.
25. Interview with Juliana Herron, Hetton-le-Hole, Durham, 20 April 1999.
26. Jerry Palmer, *Taking Humour Seriously* (London, 1994).
27. Palmer, *Taking Humour Seriously*; Mary Douglas, 'Jokes'.
28. Michael Mann, *Consciousness and Action Amongst the Western Working Class*, (London, 1973); Maxine Molyneux, 'Mobilisation without emancipation', in *Feminist Studies*, 11, 22 (summer, 1985), pp.227–51 and 'Analysing women's movements', *Development and Change*, 29 (1998), pp.219–45.
29. D.W. Livingstone and J.M. Mangan use a scale of 'radical consciousness' within which women are found to be more conservative than men in an American steel

town ('Class, gender and expanded class consciousness in Steeltown', *Research in Social Movements*, 15 (1993), pp.55–82). This approach has been criticised by feminists researching consciousness (see note 33 below).
30. In their 1991 account of mining communities David Waddington, Maggie Wykes and Chas Critcher described the women of WAPC as not having had such a great change in consciousness as that of feminists at the time. See their *Split at the Seams*, (Milton Keynes, 1991).
31. P. Abbott, 'Women's social class identification; does husband's occupation make a difference?', in *Sociology*, 21, 1 (1987), pp.91–103, K. Anderson and E. Cored, 'Women, work and political attitudes', *American Journal of Political Science*, 29, 3 (1985), pp.606–25; M. Emmison, 'Class images of "the economy": opposition and ideological incorporation within working-class consciousness', *Sociology*, 19, 1 (1985), pp.19–38; Patricia Gurin, 'Women's gender consciousness', *Public Opinion Quarterly*, 49 (1985) pp.143–63.
32. Pauline Hunt, *Gender and Class-Consciousness* (New York, 1980).
33. Anna Pollert, *Girls, Wives, Factory Lives* (London, 1981); Marilyn Porter, 'World apart: the class-consciousness of working-class women', *Women's Studies International Quarterly*, 1 (1978), pp.175–88 and *Home, Work and Class Consciousness* (Manchester, 1983).
34. Gordon Marshall, 'Some remarks on the study of working-class consciousness', *Politics and Society*, 12, 3 (1983), pp.263–301.
35. Rick Fantasia, *Cultures of Solidarity—Consciousness, Action and Contemporary American Workers* (Los Angeles, 1988).
36. Fantasia, *Cultures of Solidarity*, p.8.
37. E.P. Thompson, *Customs in Common* (New York, 1993).
38. Passerini, 'Work, ideology and working class attitudes to fascism'.
39. Marjorie Devault, 'Conflict over housework: a problem that (still) has no name', *Research in Social Movements*, 12 (1990), pp.189–202.
40. Sheila Rowbotham, 'Women's Liberation and the new politics' in Michelle Wander (ed.), *The Body Politic—Writings from the Women's Liberation Movement in Britain 1969–72* (London, 1972), p.6.

The Squatters of 1946
A local study in national context

Paul Burnham

Despite the transformations of wartime and the rhetoric of 'people's war', the Labour landslide of July 1945 came as a huge political shock. In High Wycombe, thousands had filled the high street to hear Winston Churchill speak from the massive ornate portal of the Red Lion Hotel during his election tour. Nevertheless, the voters went on to elect John Haire with a majority of 2,536 as the town's first-ever Labour MP. Squadron Leader L. John Collins, later to become a leader of the Campaign for Nuclear Disarmament, remembered that at RAF Bomber Command in High Wycombe:

> The war was practically ended, but the looks on the faces of those officers, particularly the senior ones, as it became more and more certain that the Labour Party would win a landslide victory, grew sadder and sadder. To the establishment at High Wycombe, the Labour Party victory was a disaster so overwhelming that they could hardly believe their ears. Was it for this, they seemed to be saying to themselves, that the war had been fought and won?'[1]

By stark contrast 'other ranks' everywhere rejoiced.[2]

Despite such images, writers such as Kenneth Morgan have argued that the Attlee governments of 1945–51 and their allies in the trade union leadership dominated and policed the Labour movement with relative ease.[3] Other historians have described the popular mood as one of apathy rather than activism and stressed the limited scope of political radicalism.[4] This paper presents a rather different aspect of the period. The squatters' movement that erupted all over Britain in the summer of 1946 showed a glimpse of a much less controlled working class, and one much more connected to the international wave of struggles at the war's end. As homeless families squatted in camps left disused by the armed forces, and in offices and in empty blocks of flats, domestic politics was shaken. For a moment, in the words of Michael Foot, 'the government feared widespread disorder...an outbreak of direct action which could have spread like a prairie fire'.[5] However, there has been no historical consensus as to the significance of these events. Social historians such as Susan Cooper and Paul Addison have seen the squatting as part of a painful transition towards peacetime and prosperity.[6] James Hinton's article in *History Workshop Journal*, the only academic study dedicated to the 1946 squatters, traces a path leading from the democratic and collective self-help tradition of wartime towards the later conservative hegemony of home ownership.[7] Though the intervention of the Communist Party (CP) has been positively depicted by the party's own historians, Colin Ward has celebrated the spontaneity of the squatters from an anarchist perspective which sees the involvement of the communists as wholly negative.[8] The object of this article is to take a fresh look at these issues, based not only on a survey of the available secondary materials but on a detailed case study of squatting in High Wycombe and Amersham, South Bucks.

The context of the actions may be briefly sketched. As Minister of Health in the new Labour government, Aneurin Bevan was responsible for housing, which had been one of the major issues on which Labour had own the election. Bevan prioritised council-house building and sharply restricted the private sector, but with the limited availability of labour, bricks and steel, housing progress was much slower than expected. There were additional sources of housing supply from requisitioning and from prefabrication. But with 3,500,000 servicepeople demobilised at the end of the war, extensive bomb damage, virtually no housebuilding for years past, and a sharp increase in the number of marriages and of births, the housing crisis was severe.

Bevan was passionately concerned about housing quality: 'Enough damage has already been done to the face of England by irresponsible people. I hope we shall defend housing standards. If we have to wait a little longer, that will be far better than doing ugly things now.'[9] He told his wife Jennie Lee that he thought it would have been better to build no houses in the first year or two after the war.[10] Though justified on grounds of housing standards, Labour's 'bureaucratic paternalist' attitudes meant that the role of the people was to wait.[11] It was the refusal simply to remain patient that was to give rise to the squatters' movement; indeed the major official objection to squatting was to be that the squatters were jumping the all-important waiting list.

Housing problems in High Wycombe

During the war many bombed-out families from London joined a large number of evacuees in High Wycombe. The Londoners were known as 'refugees' and 'they were poles apart in those days, they were like people from another planet'.[12] By September 1946 there were 2,400 applicants on the borough waiting list.[13] The *Bucks Free Press* reported on the 'worries of servicemen' :

> Mrs C lives with her husband in a small house containing three small bedrooms. Living with them are three sons, all demobilised after many years in the forces, and also a married daughter and her baby. The daughter's husband has been a POW, and will be demobilised at any minute. None of them can find other accommodation.
>
> Mr D is an ex-service man. He and his wife and one child live with his wife's parents in a condemned house. Living in the same house (which has two bedrooms, a kitchen and a sitting-room) are two grown-up daughters. A son in a mental hospital is fit to be discharged, and may return at any time. There is another son due for demobilisation.[14]

Even earning good money as a toolmaker at Hoovers did not help John Burnham to find a home. 'We got married when a chap from work let us have a couple of rooms in the house he was renting with his wife. There was an outside toilet and no bathroom. Everyone had to wash in the kitchen. Jimmy Bowers [from work] got married and took his wife home to his parents' house, where they slept on the landing.'[15] The 1951 census was to show that 11.5 per cent of High Wycombe's households were sharing a dwelling.[16] There were more than 4,000 houses in the town without baths, and so public slipper baths were opened in Bellfield Road.[17] The council's housing needs department told young couples 'no chance—have you got any children?'—and that was usually the end of the matter.[18]

In 1946 housing issues were argued out every week in Wycombe's local newspaper the *Bucks Free Press*. Labour councillors proposed the requisitioning for housing use of the exclusive Wycombe Abbey School. The school had been requisitioned as the headquarters of the United States Army Air Force for three years during the war, and it was claimed that at least one hundred families could be accommodated there. The Independent majority group on the Borough Council split over the Labour resolution, but the council voted by eighteen votes to seven only to 'make enquiries' about using the school for housing.[19]

Arguments about housing spilled out bitterly at a British Legion dinner in February 1946. Arthur Forward, secretary of the High Wycombe branch, advocated housing priority for ex-servicemen: 'the tendency today is to recognise people who work in factories more than the people who fought the country's battles overseas'. Major-General Sir Howard Vyse disagreed, pointedly quoting returned POWs who said 'there is something to be learnt from being a prisoner of war. We have learnt that there is some good in everybody, to have a little give-and-take, and to be tolerant.' Wycombe's Labour MP John Haire was in attendance at the dinner, but seems to have made no comment on Forward's attempt to set ex-servicemen against organised workers over the housing issue.[20]

The Tories, newly out of office, claimed that private enterprise could build houses faster than the public sector. Local builders complained of restrictive practices, agitation by a minority of workers, and 'too generous rates in the town's basic industry'.[21] The borough council called for the government to negotiate with the trade unions for longer hours in building, but the local building unions opposed overtime working on the Hatters Lane site where eighty-two new council houses were being built. The Ministry of Health agreed with the unions on overtime, but granted an Essential Works Order for the compulsory retention of labour. The union card stewards protested about poor facilities on the job: 'The 45 men on site eat in a rat infested hut seating twenty. Our lavatory consists of a pole (*sic*) to sit on, without a roof covering against bad weather.'[22] Nationally at this time, according to the history of the builders' union, 'the bricklayers in particular were put under the press microscope and abused to make a field day for readers', and by the end of 1947 the unions were forced to accept payment by results in the industry.[23]

1946 saw two major engineering strikes in High Wycombe, at Broom and Wade in April and at Cossors in October. There was also an active communist party branch in the town, which had grown through 'the people's war' and through evacuation. The wife and son of Phil Piratin, who was to become the communist MP for Mile End in 1945, were evacuated to High Wycombe and stayed with the family of local left-winger Harry Slight. Also evacuated during the war was the Thompson's trade union legal practice. Many of the solicitors were CP members, and Thompson himself was a prominent communist.[24] In 1944 Wycombe Trades Council was affiliated to the Labour Party, and sent a one-off five-member delegation to meet the CP as well.[25]

Squatting begins

There had been some isolated incidents of squatting as the war ended, and in response Churchill's 'caretaker' Conservative government of May-July 1945 allowed councils to requisition empty homes for housing need. On 8 May 1946 James Fielding began squatting at an army camp in Scunthorpe. Fielding was a cinema projectionist who with his wife and children had been sleeping in the back seats of the cinema after shows, and in the second week in August 1946 he gave a Movietone newsreel interview to explain what he had done. Mass direct action spread gradually around the country, and soon 46,000 people were occupying disused army camps, anti-aircraft gun sites and prisoner of war camps.[26] The newsreel interview had a powerful effect in spreading the action. At the time cinema audiences could react collectively and with feeling to newsreel items, and in some cinemas footage about squatting was greeted with enthusiastic applause.[27]

The squatters mainly occupied Nissen huts, which had been designed as temporary accommodation for service personnel, with roofs made of twin sheets of corrugated steel offering very limited protection from the elements. The hutted estates varied in size—some had been important military bases with hundreds of huts, while others such as anti-aircraft gun sites had only two or three. People placed a bag inside, and then chalked or padlocked the door to claim their hut. The new residents organised themselves with estate committees, and paid rent into their own funds, which were held ready for a landlord relationship to be established. There was some squatting in private property including hotels, though police action evicted the squatters from most of these sites. The Labour government was on the back foot. It claimed that the camps were unsuitable for permanent housing, and that improvement to acceptable standards would be uneconomic. However, on 17 August it announced that the squatters could stay at the hutted camps until the winter.[28] They became council tenants, though their status compared to those who had gone through the council waiting list and allocation procedures was always precarious. The phenomenon of officially encouraged or tolerated squatting began, though in the words of a War Office official: 'The strict legal position is quite clear. Nobody is allowed on Army property without the consent of the War Office'.[29] Sometimes the mood was non-political, as in Bristol where the squatters' leaders saw themselves as respectable 'homemakers'.[30] However, the involvement of the communist party was also important in many places. The communists were the only left organisation with the will or the potential to intervene in the squatters' movement. With 42,000 members compared to 645,000 individual members of the Labour Party in 1946, they shaped events in many parts of the country. In Birmingham the campaign was run from the CP office by a committee including leading CP members who were not themselves squatters, and who from the outset looked beyond army camps to the empty houses in the city.[31]

The Poles and squatting in the Amersham rural district

Aiming to limit the extent of the movement, the Labour government decided to send troops into camps that had not yet been squatted. Troops from the regular Army were used, and 91,000 troops of General Anders' Polish Army, who had declined to return to Poland, were demobilised and sent to live in some of the unoccupied camps.[32] This quick-fix solution to the two problems of squatting and of the displaced Poles brought further complications to the housing crisis. Many homeless families, including those not yet squatting, were outraged, and the communist party, recognising Anders as an enemy of the post-war government in Poland, encouraged this reaction. The sharpest confrontations over this issue came in South Bucks:

> A chance word spoken in Chalfont St Giles on Saturday evening had repercussions throughout the country.
>
> Mr Bailey, a craftsman living with his wife in circumstances far from ideal, happened to over hear on Saturday at half-past six that Poles and their Italian wives were shortly to take up occupation at the Vache Camp, which stands on the high ground overlooking the village. He got busy and conveyed the news to several friends who were living in like conditions and three hours later he with six other families had taken possession of some of the camp huts.
>
> In the war he and one or two of his comrades in this venture were Commandos, and having been taught to take risks, they took this one. He told our reporter:
>
> 'I walked about six miles telling people of the opportunity that was awaiting them and from then on there has been a gradual trek of people from the village, from Chalfont St Peter, Rickmansworth, and in consequence from wide publicity, from such far distant places as Chelmsford, Oxford and Banstead.'[33]

The story of five hundred Italian brides of Polish soldiers on their way to the area, with a shopping centre, theatre and cinema to be installed for their benefit, certainly played on national and sexual anxieties. The 'Italian brides' were in fact Polish women who had married Polish soldiers in Italy.[34] In any case local squatters occupied sixty-five huts at the Vache, and ten days later Poles moved into another forty-two huts there. In the meantime fifty local families and thirty Polish troops moved into Hazlemere Park Camp in Wycombe Rural District. One of the squatters there, former militiaman Mr L. Austin, said 'I have wired my wife in Liverpool and she is coming here. I have only seen her for two weeks since I was demobbed two months ago, and I have been sleeping in the hall of my mother's bungalow'.[35]

According to a *Daily Worker* report, at Beech Barn in Chesham Bois:

> A Polish officer ordered his men to spread themselves out through the empty huts—to live one to a hut. But eight families 'evicted' them to obtain their new homes. They simply retrieved the beds while the Poles looked on in silence. The Poles were also busy erecting barbed wire around the remaining huts and taking up 'defence' positions. Polish soldiers also arrived at a camp at Piper's Wood, Hyde Heath, near Chesham, when squatters occupied it yesterday afternoon.[36]

Although hands-on physical confrontations seem to have been avoided, the mood was very hostile to the Poles. Chalfont St Peter Residents' Association wanted them housed in isolated camps on Salisbury Plain or in Cornwall.[37] 'The huts should have been let to English people a long time ago' was one comment from Vache Park, and leading local communist Elizabeth Leigh 'had strong objections to the Poles in the district'. With the slogans 'Amersham camps for Amersham people' and 'Beech Barn for the British', a delegation of squatters visited Downing Street to demand the eviction of the Poles.[38] The few kind words about them came from the middle class and the political right, in the form of two letters to the *Bucks Free Press* and comments from some Independent councillors in Amersham.

The 'United Front' and squatting in Wycombe

Squatting in High Wycombe began at the former Italian prisoner-of-war camp in Chairborough Road in the third week in August. The Italians had been the subject of much local curiosity, both at the camp and while taking their regular weekly exercise through the town accompanied by soldiers.[39] When the Italians had left in May 1946, the camp had been badly vandalised. Although the borough council had declared the huts 'completely unfit for habitation', squatters repaired some of the damage at their own expense. Some of the money was later repaid from central government funds, though in the first week Mr. S.C.Mansbridge had already spent £12 on materials. 'If I could buy one of these huts at a reasonable price, I would be prepared to spend money to make it habitable' was the comment of his father. Around the squatters 'the rest of the camp presents a scene of desolation—every pane of glass in the huts has been smashed, stoves are damaged beyond repair and holes have been knocked in some of the roofs.'[40]

The most important site in High Wycombe was Daws Hill in the grounds of Wycombe Abbey. It was one of the biggest camps in the country with 220 Nissen huts. The story of squatting at Daws Hill has been recorded by local communist activist Jack Spector:

> Word was passed round to prospective squatters in High Wycombe and the surrounding villages, and on the specified day, with co-ordinated timing, CP members, with the Labour Party supporters they could muster, went to the main gate and cut the wires that had been attached to them. Within a very short time, the first squatters arrived from the foot of Daws Hill, with their bedding, their belongings and their families. It was first come, first served in obtaining the best quarters. Before long there was a steady stream of squatters ascending Daws Hill, and by the evening there were two hundred and more people in the camp.[41]

The involvement of Labour Party members alongside communists was a pronounced feature in High Wycombe. The *Daily Worker* reported that the proposal to requisition the Abbey School had been 'a Communist Party suggestion'.[42] An effective campaign against rent increases for the 700 Wycombe Rural District Council tenants was another 'united front' project in 1947, when a petition initiated by Jack Spector as a communist parish councillor was circulated with the assistance of members of the communist and Labour parties.[43]

However there was another side to this picture of communist initiative. The Labour Party member June Parrymore insists that the squat was the initiative of Wally Wright and her father Harry Slight, both also Labour Party members, while Jack Spector and Ray Russell 'drifted in and out of the Labour Party and the Communist Party.'[44] She says that the CP may well have been involved in promoting the requisitioning of Wycombe Abbey as Jack Spector and Cllr. Bob Darby knew one another well. Harry Slight was a furniture worker who had returned from service as a medic in India in 1945 to be told by his wife that 'you'll have to decide which way to go, because if you join the Communist Party I won't come with you.' Harry said that he had already decided to join Labour.[45] Wally Wright was a former miner who had been sacked and imprisoned after the 1932 Bedwas Navigation Colliery strike in South Wales.[46] In 1936 Wally rode to Wycombe on his bicycle with a shilling in his pocket, and since 1939 he had been an AEU member working at Broom and Wade.[47] In 1946 Wally was living in a multigenerational household headed by his mother, with his new partner Flo and her daughter Joyce who were evacuees from London, one of his brothers (two more were in the forces), one of his brothers' wives, and two lodgers.[48]

Whoever was really driving the 'united front', cutting the wire at Daws Hill on 31 August was a joint operation. The communists Ron and Marian Williams were the first Daws Hill squatters alongside Wally and Flo Wright.[49] Wally Wright's belongings were ferried uphill to the camp in a large black Austin driven by Horace Aylwin, the Labour councillor who as AEU convenor had recently led 700 workers in the Broom and Wade's strike.[50] The communist party provided legal support, perhaps through the Thompson's legal practice.[51] Harry Slight's sons write that 'as all the political folk were intermingled (Communists and Labour) I can't remember anyone being more than the other' and 'to my recollection they were in a large majority of cases one and the same.'[52]

Although Daws Hill 'was a beautiful site…bigger and better than the other camps because it was an American camp', the squatters faced the immediate problem of getting facilities organised.[53] Telegraph poles were cut down and used for fuel. The camp had been in the process of decommissioning and the water supply had been switched off, but the novelist and communist party member Elizabeth Taylor lived nearby and helped out with buckets of water.[54] John Haire MP attended a conference with council, school and ministry officers on the first weekend of the Daws Hill squat, and gradually services were laid on, but Brenda Barnett remembers 'that first winter, my hands were raw.' She spent whole afternoons shifting coke in an old pram, and at night heard mice running between the two sheets of corrugated tin inside the roof of her hut.[55] Wyn Hawes remembers that 'it was damp and very, very cold…when my son came out of hospital, I knitted a hat for him to wear indoors, but he was still cold.'[56]

The London squatters, Bevan and the Communist Party

The national context of the squatting campaign now decisively shaped local events. On Sunday 8 September, just a week after Wally Wright, Ron Williams and their families moved into Daws Hill, the Communist Party stepped up the action by organising the squatting of five blocks of luxury flats in central London. These had been derequisitioned and offered to councils for housing use, but still stood empty. The response of the Labour government was to forbid the provision of any services, and then to charge five communist councillors with 'conspiracy to trespass'. The police laid siege to Abbey Lodge, one of the luxury blocks, while crowds sat down in the road, and the squatters responded by singing 'there'll always be an England'. This took place in the main road on the West Side of Regent's Park, in the full glare of national publicity.[57]

Remarkably, this escalation, which put squatting at the centre of national politics, was an initiative of the London district of the communist party, taken when Harry Pollitt, the party's general secretary, was out of London. When they met determined opposition from the Labour government, the communists decided to end the London squatting after only ten days. They backed down so quickly because in 1946 the CP was following an approach of 'critical support' of Labour and did not want a head-on challenge to the government. The London squatting had been targeted not at Labour, but at the Tory councils of Kensington and Westminster that had refused to accept the requisitioned properties for housing use. In its housing work the communist party focused on Aneurin Bevan, addressing him as a friend and comrade, and presenting the squatting as supportive of Labour's housing policy.[58]

The feeling however was not reciprocated. When a delegation from the London Trades Council met him on 18 September, Bevan took a hard line. He expressed his sympathy for those living in bad conditions—but certainly not for the squatters.[59] Bevan's political weekly *Tribune* published a brazen front page editorial 'Help Yourself to a Leg of Lamb!' equating the squatters with common thieves.[60] Frederic Mullaley has described how 'all the inside political stuff' in *Tribune* 'came from Nye and Michael Foot, who increasingly wrote the leaders after Nye became a minister.' Bevan often attended the Monday morning conferences, sometimes making an impromptu political speech.[61] 'Help Yourself to a Leg of Lamb!' therefore shows just how badly the Labour politicians, even of the left, were shaken by the squatting campaign. Anti-communism was a useful stick with which to beat back the rising movement of direct action. No wonder that James Hinton believes that the squatting campaign was unhelpful to the communist party's perspective of 'brokerage', based on both leading and managing working class discontent with the government, and on the occasional quiet chat between leading CP members and Labour MPs.[62]

The communist party's friendly orientation towards Bevan was uneasily combined with sharp criticism of him for clamping down on the London protesters. The coverage in the *Daily Worker*, and the notes for Harry Pollitt's speech in Leicester Square during the London squatters crisis, with their many revisions and changes of emphasis, show the difficulties of this contradictory line. Pollitt's speech blew hot and cold in relation to Bevan, and spoke loosely of possible industrial action in support of the squatters. On the servicemen he strikingly quoted Kipling's *Tommy Atkins*:

> It's Tommy this, an' Tommy that, an' chuck him out, the brute,
> But it's 'saviour of his country' when the guns begin to shoot

It's Tommy this an' Tommy that, an' anything you please
But Tommy ain't a blooming fool, you bet that Tommy sees!

followed by the stirring call 'let us have a little bit of Britain for the British to be going on with.'[63]

Like *The Grand Old Duke of York*, the CP marched their army up the hill—and then marched them down again. After the end of the campaign, they claimed the London squatting as a great victory, with positive changes in housing policy from both councils and government. There was some truth in this, as the squatting had been a disorienting shock to Labour. However after mid-September the political tide went out on the housing question, leaving the 46,000 camp squatters if not stranded, at least with a much softer focus for their struggles.

Life in the camps: Amersham

Squatters were 'the flavour of the month' in August 1946, and in Amersham the passengers of passing buses 'craned their necks to see any new developments on the camps'.[64] With the patriotic profile of squatting very prominent in Amersham, the coverage in the *Bucks Examiner* was not just favourable but positively lyrical. Amersham rural district council (RDC) then settled down to deal with the new and unusual situation. On 16 August a meeting was held between the council and army officers, and referring to the stories about the Italian brides, Colonel G.B. Aris said 'an incorrect impression had been created'. In fact there would as usual be married quarters for 5 per cent of the military personnel. The army representatives claimed that the camps were still required for military purposes, although they had been empty for months, and the council had been trying in vain to get them released for housing.[65]

As in Wycombe, life in the camps was very hard at first. Elizabeth Barry had been living in a caravan with her two children, her brother, his wife, and their little girl, and 'things were not going well, the caravan being small'. So the family moved to Beech Barn, at first living in spartan conditions on the stage of the camp's dance hall, with blankets strung up for some limited privacy. Although this was supposedly a council-managed site from the beginning, in 1946 and 1947 there was no council control over allocation. Instead either the camp committee decided, or else 'squatter's rights' applied. On one occasion when squatters went to find friends to move into a hut that had suddenly become available, they followed them to a cinema, where the manager agreed to flash a message onto the screen telling the couple to go to claim their new home. From the dance hall stage Elizabeth's family moved—quickly between the patrol duties of the Polish troops—into a very basic Nissen hut with more blankets as internal walls. They had to wait until Spring 1948 until the council allocated them a renovated hut at the camp. As well as corrugated tin huts, Beech Barn also had wooden and corrugated asbestos huts.[66] Elizabeth's son Dave James writes that 'a firm friendship developed amongst us all, soldiers and families alike'. Elizabeth's worst job was gathering firewood in the winter. When troops were moving out of Pipers Wood camp in 1947, the Polish soldiers helped the Beech Barn squatters to shift furniture and rolls of lino all evening between the two camps in carts, prams, trollies and pushchairs.[67]

> Mrs Margaret Ward lived in one of the concrete blocks at Vache Park: There was no indoor plumbing—it was all very rough up there. There was a water standpipe fifty yards away in the middle of a field, and 10–15 yards away was a big toilet block. There were improvements later, but not until after two years. In 1947 when we had the big freeze it was really cold. I was a little girl and the snow came up to my waist—I thought I was going to disappear! The standpipe froze and we tried to unfreeze it using just matches. We had to go outside to go from one of our rooms into the other. Excuse my language, but in the cold weather my dad said 'sod it' and knocked a hole through, and put up a dividing curtain. There was some heating inside, from a big pot-bellied stove. We had two primus stoves to cook with. We had a tin bath heated by the primus stove, but that was only once a week.[68]

Council officers were concerned to keep new squatters out of the camps, but they were often unsuccessful. At Vache Park new squatters moved in when huts were vacated temporarily for estate improvements.[69] At Penn Street Common contractors went to remove demolish empty huts but 'owing to insufficient despatch' found them occupied by new squatters.[70]

When Amersham council prosecuted 'unauthorised squatters' in August 1947, the result was less than straightforward. Squatter children prattled and wandered in the courtroom, and followed their mothers to the witness box.[71] The county court judge requested the council to assist the squatters with their housing problems.[72] One of the accused was Daisy Hunt. She had moved from an overcrowded cottage at Chesham Vale into Beech Barn Camp with her husband and baby:

> I still have court summons papers…We all eventually were all took to court, and the outcome was, our huts were made into proper rooms. Two bedrooms bathroom & toilet. Kitchen with usual tops also copper to boil our clothes etc. Also a 'long' living room with a wood and coal cooking

range which had to keep all the rooms warm. It was fine as none of us had lived in centrally heated homes then…I had two more babies whilst living there both born in the hut. We all lived happily enough and to me it was heaven having my man working with me to make something of a life for our children.[73]

There was effective collective action by squatters at Pipers Wood Camp in 1949. The council had refused to adopt this site, claiming that it was unsuitable for housing. Councillor Captain Bouquet, chairman of the housing committee, called it a 'priority clearing house to get houses in this district' used by people 'some even from Devon.'[74] This provoked bitter protests. The front page of the *Bucks Examiner* was given over to angry letters from Mr. R.G. Ward of the Pipers Wood tenants' committee, Elizabeth Leigh of Amersham Communist Party, and Ward's father. A public meeting was addressed by Ward and Leigh, and the CP arranged for communist MP Phil Piratin to question Aneurin Bevan about Pipers Wood in the House of Commons. The council agreed to take over twenty-nine of the huts, and then to take over the site with forty huts, and then to allocate £9,457 for improvements.[75] The CP was also active at Beech Barn where according to Elizabeth Barry 'most of us joined the communist party as they were fighting the council to provide us with gas cookers—without success I might add'.[76] In February 1949 the communists were holding a regular weekly advice surgery, and in the May 1949 RDC elections took 6.5 per cent of the vote in Amersham ward.[77]

Amersham RDC expanded its housing stock by adopting the Polish camps at Woodlands Park and Hodgemoor as well as Pipers Wood, and by converting and dividing the huts. £36,336 came from the national Exchequer for camp conversions between February 1949 and March 1950. From a prewar base of 666 council houses, by March 1950 the Rural District's stock had increased to a total of 1,496 homes, including 333 postwar houses, 90 prefabs, 52 requisitioned properties, and 355 dwellings in seven hutted camps including two former anti-aircraft sites.[78]

The paternalism of the British social administrative tradition adds its full flavour to the council minutes for this period. The squatters are variously described as campers, accepted squatters, tenants, and occupants, while their homes change from estates to camps and then back again. In June 1947, Captain Bouquet, backed by a statement from the Ministry of Health, was concerned to end representation by the residents' committee at Vache Park: the watchword was the maintenance of full official 'control'.[79] By 1953 a government circular was prodding councils towards closure of the camps.

The huts at Vache Park were declared a danger to public health as 'there was hardly a family on the estate that did not need a doctor in the winter.'[80] Demolition took place throughout 1954, and the last tenants left in May 1955.[81] Beech Barn closed in 1956. The last site to close was Hodgemoor, where the very last tenants did not leave until 1962.[82]

Amersham council was troubled into the late 1950s by new squatters and by rogue tenants who would not leave to allow for site closures. Eviction cases in March 1956 led to delicate negotiations between Amersham RDC and Buckinghamshire county council. The County did not want children being left homeless, and wanted 'a chance to try to educate the defaulting parents in the care of houses and the payment of rents and arrears' while Amersham 'would not contemplate allocating council houses to the type of person concerned.' As a compromise, one tenant was evicted at Beech Barn and one at Pipers Wood in the hope of a salutary effect on the other defaulting tenants.[83] An unauthorised squatter at Hodgemoor was evicted in May 1956, but it emerged that a housing committee member had told him: 'Go ahead and squat. It is your only chance. You will probably be taken to a Magistrate's Court and fined £2, and that is all.'[84]

Life in the camps: Wycombe

Not everyone was pleased to see the arrival of working-class people, and especially the 'great male unwashed', at Daws Hill. Wycombe Abbey School had reopened on 9 May 1946 after the departure of the US Army Air Force. When the squatting began Miss Crosthwaite, the Headmistress, spoke of 'the action of certain persons, acting apparently under leadership and by arrangement'. According to the school magazine 'her economical statement conceals the considerable anxiety that this circumstance caused. She had faced the fact that some parents might be unwilling to let their daughters return, and although this fear was not realised, she had had to brace herself for such an outcome'. The beginning of term was postponed until after 'the erection of an impassable fence' between the school and the camp.[85] Some other local residents were also unhappy. As a child David Williams lived opposite the camp. He was threatened with a block of wood by a squatter child, and he says that the squatters 'were jealous of the people in Daws Hill Lane who in turn resented the presence of some rather dubious characters'.[86] Pamela Goodwin's father was an active supporter of the squatters:

> We had some chickens in our garden at Keep Hill, and somebody broke in at night and stole them—and my father went up to the camp and recognised

his chickens. So some of them didn't know who was their benefactor.[87]

The joint presence of Labour and communist party members continued to feature at Daws Hill. 'The squatters were of course a highly organised and politically conscious group. During their time at Daws Hill they collectively worked to improve their conditions and pressurised the council to give them help' writes Trevor Fowler.[88] Improvements at the Daws Hill Estate were a preoccupation of the housing committee, and in January 1947 the Ministry of Health approved an estimate for work costing £15,047.[89] This was at a time when a new permanent council house cost about £1,200. The huts were painted and partitioned into living and bedroom spaces, new baths were provided and sinks installed, and private toilet facilities for each hut were introduced to replace the communal ablution blocks. A full-time resident warden was employed, with a coin-operated telephone for the use of the residents.[90]

Wally Wright became the chairman and the only non-communist member of the camp committee.[91] Ron Williams stood in the November 1946 council elections under the proud label 'Building Worker, Squatter, Communist', winning 280 votes, exactly half of the Labour poll, and the support of around 15 per cent of the voters.[92] George Fairbairn was another of the squatters. Before the war he had been the chauffeur to the Hoovers MD Sir Charles Colston. He had unionised Hoovers during the war and made it a closed shop, and he lived at Daws Hill with Mary Meeks who was the overseer of the women who made switchgear at Hoovers.[93] In December 1946 the first Daws Hill social evening, with its extensive variety of performances, took place by the light of oil lamps, compered by Ron Williams and attended by Wycombe's Labour MP John Haire.[94] The CP brought the Workers Theatre to Daws Hill to perform, and produced the *Daws Hill Despatch* as a bulletin for the camp.[95]

> Ernest Barnett remembers the squatters dispensing some rough justice: We had some travellers you'd call them now—gypsies who took a hut up there, across the far side of the camp. We ignored them for a week or so, but they messed the place up, didn't bother going to the toilet but just did it outside the hut. We had a committee meeting and decided to get them out. One Sunday morning we got them out. We had the police there, but we did it ourselves.[96]

The huts leaked, and in 1949 their roofs were waterproofed by Bitumen Industries Ltd. Many of them leaked again and were condemned, but the Borough Council was still rehousing people at the camp in 1951. As families were allocated houses and the huts were demolished, facilities at the camp were gradually withdrawn. As the US Army Air Force returned to the site, the camp closed in 1953.

Like all the squatted camps, this was a young community and a refreshing break from multigenerational housing. 'It was a lovely atmosphere, everyone got on well. It was a very close community', remembers Joyce Hadfield.[97] Wyn Hawes adds: 'There wasn't older people there, their husbands had just come out of the forces. The children were all under school age, or just starting school. We made lots of friends. I was lucky as my dad had a big allotment.'[98] Ernest and Brenda Barnett also remember the good times, like a 'holiday camp in the summer', with 'lovely tea parties' and 'the women…walking about in just their bras and shorts'. They also remembered how proud they were to be squatters. As Ernest Barnett puts it: 'We made homes for ourselves, and by doing it we took a lot of pressure off the council. I've never been ashamed of being a squatter, I've often been proud of it, at least we made something for ourselves and didn't rely on other people.'[99]

The Polish presence

After 1946 Poles and local squatters shared the camps in South Bucks. Hostility to the Polish presence had been an important factor in the summer of 1946, certainly in Amersham, but as things slowly changed, the labour movement resisted bitterly. Phil Piratin was evidently the MP for every CP branch in the south of England. This time supplied with information from High Wycombe, in 1948 he asked George Isaacs, the Minister of Labour, why Poles were working as barmen, waiters and porters at the Red Lion Hotel. He claimed that Polish musicians had been playing there 'taking the place of a band, all the members of which belong to the Musicians Union'. Two Conservative MPs intervened to protest at the obvious malice behind his question, but Piratin labelled them as supporters of 'scab labour', and he was able to secure new guidelines restricting the musical activities of residents of the Polish camps.[100] As legislation forbade the use of Polish labour to replace British workers, those hostile to the Poles were in a strong position to prevent their employment.

This was not just a communist party campaign. At both its November and December 1946 meetings, Wycombe Trades Council resolved to seek the early return of all Poles to Poland at the earliest opportunity.[101] By 1949 with the cold war in full swing, George Fairbairn, squatter, Labour Party member, shop steward at Hoovers, and president of High Wycombe No.2 AEU branch, was advising members to vote against communists in union elections, and opposing any support for strikes led by CP members.[102] Until 1948 the AEU had excluded Poles from membership, but once the rules had changed, Hoovers wanted to employ Polish women.[103] George Fairbairn however was reluctant to comply, and he raised the Polish question at the branch meeting of 7 April 1949. He mentioned the Jalpatex factory in Slough where Polish women had remained at work whilst British workers were on strike, and another member added that Polish women were still employed at Cossors while redundancies were occurring. By 2 June however Fairbairn was proposing the admission to the branch of two women 'who were Polish nationals and working at Hoovers, as no English girls were available to fill the jobs'. The bottom line was that 'if we did not admit them the T&GWU would'.[104] It is notable that there was no recorded opposition, right or left, in such meetings to the position of 'send them back, or keep them out'.[105] June Parrymore remembers that 'I was told to keep away from them at dances, "don't you get involved with one of them" and so on. I'm sure it was my dad who thought they were right-wing.'[106]

Life in the camps dedicated solely to Poles was harsh. Hodgemoor had been a Polish hostel run by the National Assistance Board. When it was taken over by Amersham RDC in 1950 for Polish families only, seventeen single Poles refused to leave and were taken to court. Communal feeding arrangements at the hostel had recently been abolished, and the residents issued with ration books, but they still slept in dormitories and had no private bedrooms or furniture. The judge informed the defendants that their housing had been 'an arrangement that could be put an end to when and for whatever reason' the National Assistance Board decided.[107]

Edna Burnham remembers that many Poles, Ukrainians and Yugoslavs worked at Cossors factory at Loudwater. They lived in the hostel at Flackwell Heath, they used to walk down through the woods to work, and 'the Polish men did menial jobs like the jobs that the girls did'.[108] In the camps there was a gradual thaw in attitudes. Dave James, who grew up at Beech Barn, records plenty of good times with the Polish troops there. When Dave's mother Elizabeth was divorced in 1947, she married a Polish soldier at the camp.[109]

Hazlemere Park Camp, shared by Poles and local squatters in 1946, became from 1947 a Polish Resettlement Camp. A Polish school was with fifty-four preschool, primary and secondary students.[110] Stella Downes remembers:

> It was all Poles who lived there, and they made a lovely little village of it. They even made their own church out of two Nissen huts knocked together, out of bits and pieces and whatever was to hand. They kept the gardens beautiful.[111]

Mr and Mrs. Wylot lived in a hut under a conker tree where 'it was like gunshots at night'.[112] The village historian records both Poles and locals enjoying a craft exhibition at the camp at Christmas 1948. There was another camp nearby at St. John's. This was a hostel with 400 Poles in 1947, living eight to a Nissen hut.[113] In 1949 St John's, then with 45 huts housing returning POWs and unmarried Poles, was taken over by Wycombe Rural District Council, but it was decided that the village did not need two Polish camps.

Although this was not the first migration from outside the British Isles, there was at first little understanding for the Poles. They found greater acceptance as time passed, but communists, trade unionists and Labour Party members played a consistently negative role. It is true that many of the Poles were right-wing, and it was also true that a few of them had 'fought for Hitler' at some stage during the war. However the left failed to engage with the reasons why such things had happened. Confusion and denial about the uncomfortable reality of events in Eastern Europe blended with a narrow-minded opposition to competition from foreign labour. The response to the Polish migrants is not an episode that reflects any credit on the left.

Mr Marian Wylot describes the impact of labour and housing controls on Polish workers. 'I was demobbed in April 1947 on six months probation, and we had to sign a contract. The jobs that were given to us were railways, building sites and mining, because the trade unions would not accept us, as we were "fascists" in those days'. Mr Wylot left his building job to work at Jacksons paper mill. The same night he was evicted from St. John's hostel by the Squadron Leader who ran it: 'I suppose the Labour Exchange had phoned him up.' Mr Jackson took Marian to a place in the much more habitable brick-built civilian hostel at Flackwell Heath.

> I joined the trade union, and then they made me machine manager. I had five men under me, and the Jacksons workforce went out on strike. The General Secretary of the Papermakers Union came down and said 'you can't go on strike against your own member'.

He married Maria in 1949, and they lived happily for three years at Hazlemere Park Camp. The couple were allocated a council house at Flackwell Heath in 1952 or 1953, but 'the rent collector called me names because I got a council house when English families were living in barracks. So we saved money and bought a house. We lived there [Flackwell Heath] ten months only.'[114]

In High Wycombe there were examples of hutted camps becoming the stigmatised 'runt-end' of public housing provision.[115] After 1951 the Chairborough Road camp was used as temporary accommodation for the homeless in a project funded by several local councils. When the tenants protested about their miserable living conditions in September 1952, rents were reduced from £1 to 17s. 6d a week. However Buckinghamshire county council still refused tenants the right to use their own furniture, while Beaconsfield UDC saw the camp as housing for 'subnormal tenants'.[116] The site was finally closed and de-requisitioned in March 1956. In similar vein, Trevor Fowler remembers that High Wycombe Borough Council also housed homeless people in disused army huts in Cock Lane in the 1950s, 'but the conditions there were scandalously bad'.[117]

The squatters in perspective: self-help or direct action?

The housing question had enormous resonance in the Britain of the 1940s. The rule of the marketplace, and the customary polite methods of peacetime, had been suspended for six years. The ex-servicemen were the most radicalised group in society, and they were central to the strength of feeling and the organisation behind the squatting campaigns. Squatting worked across a blurred line between legality and illegality, and direct action won a degree of acceptance in cases of necessity.[118] There was plenty of potential for a much more uncompromising fight over housing, but here the politics of the communist party were crucial. If the Communist Party had made a stand in defence of the besieged London squatters, they could have spread the message effectively through the squatted camps in places like South Bucks. The CP was working alongside Labour Party and trade union allies with real roots amongst home-seekers, in the workplaces and in the community. The strike leader ferrying the belongings of the squatters up to Daws Hill, the activists of the Communist and Labour parties who were 'one and the same', the county courtroom full of roaming children helping to get their parents rehoused: all these speak to us of possibilities that went unrealised.

During the war when they opposed strikes, the communists had become expert in mobilising flexible and effective pressure in the workplace.[119] Some real meaning could have been given to Harry Pollitt's words: 'the working class is in fighting mood. It will not stand idly by and see its fellow workers brutally thrown out of their present abodes.'[120] It has been suggested that as the CP had no such perspective, this line of argument has no validity.[121] This is a debatable question, but Richard Croucher's reference to the enormous industrial debt 'owed by the British governing class to their ostensible political enemies' could equally be applied to housing.[122] Sadly for the left the Communist Party was 'the only game in town' and the tiny forces to its left could neither pose an effective ideological alternative to the CP nor intervene independently in the squatting campaign.[123]

On the other hand, given that after the end of the squatting of luxury flats, the communist party took the movement into a protracted struggle conducted at a much lower pitch, how can we assess the effectiveness of the party's strategy of brokerage, considered on its own terms? It seems evident that the London events severely damaged the kind of relationships the CP was attempting to build. The evidence from South Bucks about the effect of the camp squatting however is less clear. I have not been able to interview any of the leading squatters or local political activists from 1946, though some may still be alive. However, the respectable votes cast in local elections for Ron Williams and Elizabeth Leigh demonstrate the resonance of their campaigning in working class communities. In Amersham the communists worked with little reference to the local Labour Party, and as people moved into council houses, the relevance of work based on the squatted estates must inevitably have faded. In Wycombe both Labour and Communist parties had members and influence. However the Labour government's record, with a million new permanent homes of which 79 per cent were council properties, the introduction of the NHS, and with the added impact of the cold war, helped to marginalise the communist party.[124] Noreen Branson, its official historian, described the general election of February 1950 as 'one of the worst setbacks in the party's history'. Elizabeth Leigh was the communist candidate for Wycombe, taking only 199 votes (0.4%), the lowest share of the vote of any candidate in the entire General Election.[125] The key communist activists of 1946 were no longer members of the High Wycombe CP branch by the mid-1950s. The branch had then about twenty-thirty members but its activities were 'very little.' Ron Williams was chairman of the trades council in the late 1950s but he and Marian had left the party by then.[126]

The Labour Party reaped the political benefits of the squatting campaign. In Wycombe, Harry Slight became a borough councillor in 1949, Wally Wright in 1952, and George Fairbairn in 1954. Trevor Fowler comments:

> Certainly Wally and Bob Darby must have learned a lot about housing policy in that time, and when they were on the council, housing was the absolute number one priority for them…Wally and Bob used to have the most fearful rows, but Bob Darby had built up a land bank to build council houses on. When I came on the council with Wally [in 1970] we didn't have enough building land, and Wally was always quoting what Bob had done.[127]

The twist, however, was that by the early 1950s, national policy was shaped by a Conservative government that cut room size specifications, introduced subsidies for high flats instead of houses, and began the residualisation of council housing.[128] Even under Labour, there had been battles over standards. Despite protests from the local CP and the trades council, the ceiling clearances of new council houses in Amersham were dropped from 8ft to 7ft 6ins.[129] In Wycombe 'duplex' flats were built ready for conversion as houses when housing conditions eased, but the conversions never happened.[130] Nationally the provision of upstairs and downstairs toilets in new council houses was scrapped not by the Tories, but under Labour after Bevan left housing in January 1951. The successes of Labour councillors like Bob Darby and Wally Wright were trapped within a policy framework that was sliding in the opposite direction. The council housing boom was predicated on a capitalist boom that in the long run was not to last.

What happened to the contradictions within Labour Party attitudes? How much tension was there between the Labour Party members who supported the squatters, and Aneurin Bevan making his impromptu speech in the *Tribune* editorial offices denouncing them? The answer is probably very little. Camp squatting did not pose such a challenge to the government as squatting in luxury flats, and in time Labour policies permitted a rapid expansion of council housing. Furthermore I think we can say that although the communist party operated in less and less favourable circumstances from the late 1940s onwards, it failed at any time to address the contradictions within Labour's working class base. Despite its shifts of perspective, it lacked an orientation on the serious grassroots activists, still loyal to Labour, who were actively involved alongside the communists in places like Wycombe.

In some ways the camp squatters of 1946 made a virtue out of necessity. The camps were young communities, though their hardships meant that the squatters had necessarily exchanged one kind of communal life for another. They found something better than the multigenerational houses that were then common, something better than Jimmy Bowers starting married life on his parents' landing. As one squatter remembers: 'It was freedom…you could have a right good row, it was heaven on earth'.[131] Many separated or remarried parents lived in the camps, alongside young couples who had declined to wait for years before starting their families. The camps offered space for the initiatives of women: one Bucks squatter writes 'Doug knew nothing about our going to the Vache…I went over to Chalfont St. Giles and staked my claim.'[132] Some squatters were people brought into the area by the war, or who had taken the opportunity to move as the war ended. The Daws Hill squatters 'came from the town, perhaps not many were from Wycombe originally, but they had been in the town during the war.'[133] Margaret Ward's parents came from Scotland for a post-demobilisation holiday: 'My mum fell in love with Bucks and didn't want to go home.'[134]

The bold initiatives of the squatters are seen by Colin Ward as distinct from the passivity and dependency of other tenants, and by James Hinton as opening the way to conservative individualism.[135] They might be traced in Mr Mansbridge at Chairborough Road, and in Ernest Barnett's comments on self-reliance and dealing with travellers at Daws Hill. In fact there was a heady cocktail of 'making-do', enterprise and class struggle, though no sufficient vehicle for the latter was present. If we can avoid projecting later developments back to 1946, the postwar experience can critically inform our view of the present. Today, when many people enjoy more privacy and more space for personal life, housing developments have also created many more uncomfortable and challenging spaces for the working class and the poor.

The squatting worked. Councils were obliged to provide housing for those they saw as outsiders and queue jumpers, and to address them as the representatives of a legitimate interest in society. The squatters put pressure on government and councils to keep housing high on the policy agenda. Many of them had a lot of fun along the way. Almost all the squatters moved from the camps into council housing, at a time when council housing was a tenure of preference for working people, and when most households (53 per cent in 1950) were still renting privately.[136]

The postwar squatters remind us of the varying forms that class struggles can take. In 1946 the housing question had the potential to focus a challenge to the Attlee government. If camp squatting ultimately blended back into the Labour mainstream, the dynamics of the movement suggest that alternative outcomes were possible.

Notes
1. Canon L.John Collins, *Faith Under Fire* (London, 1966), pp.89–90.
2. Willam Harrington and Peter Young, *The 1945 Revolution* (London, 1978), p.190.
3. Kenneth O Morgan, *Labour in Power 1945–1951* (Oxford), 1984, chs 2 and 7.
4. See e.g. Steven Fielding, Peter Thompson and Nick Tiratsoo, *'England Arise!' The Labour Party and popular politics in 1940s Britain* (Manchester, 1995); for a critique, see James Hinton, '1945 and the Apathy School', *History Workshop Journal*, 43 (1997), pp.266–73.
5. Michael Foot, *Aneurin Bevan 1945–1960* (London, 1973), pp.80–81.
6. Susan Cooper, 'Snoek Piquante: the trials and tribulations of the housewife' in Michael Sissons and Philip French (eds), *Age of Austerity* (London, 1963); Paul Addison, *Now The War is Over* (London, 1985).
7. James Hinton, 'Self-help and socialism: the squatters' movement of 1946',

History Workshop Journal, 25 (1988), pp.100–26.
8. See Noreen Branson, *London Squatters 1946* (London, 1989); Colin Ward, 'Direct action for houses: the story of the squatters', *Anarchy*, 23 (1963).
9. Richard A. Sabatino, *Housing Policy in Great Britain 1945–49* (Dallas, 1956), p.10.
10. Jennie Lee, *My Life with Nye* (London, 1963), p.158.
11. Hinton, 'Self-help and socialism', p.100.
12. Interview with Pamela Goodwin, 6 April 2003.
13. *Bucks Free Press*, 20 September 1946.
14. *Bucks Free Press*, 8 February 1946.
15. Interview with John Burnham, 13 June 2002.
16. Census 1951, Bucks County Report, p.xxviii.
17. *Bucks Free Press*, 21 February 1947.
18. Interview with Edna Burnham, 13 June 2002.
19. High Wycombe borough council housing committee minutes (High Wycombe Public Library), 18 December 1945; *Bucks Free Press*, 28 December 1945.
20. *Bucks Free Press*, 22 February 1946.
21. Phil Eldridge, *Bucks Free Press*, 21 March 1947; Councillor A. Becket, *Bucks Free Press*, 24 January 1947.
22. Letter from R. Foster and P.P.A. Hodgson, AUBTW and TGWU card stewards, *Bucks Free Press*, 9 August 1946. 'Pole' is in the original. Perhaps the toilet was a 'pail' however.
23. W.S. Hilton, Foes to Tyranny: A History of the Amalgamated Union of Building Trade Workers (London, 1963), pp.268–9.
24. Interview with Trevor Fowler, 23 April 2003.
25. Wycombe Trades Union Council minutes (High Wycombe Public Library) 1935–46.
26. Hinton, 'Self-help', p.104; Nicholas Timmins, *The Five Giants* (London, 2001 edn), p.144.
27. See Hinton, 'Self-help', n.65.
28. *Labour Research*, November 1946, p.163.
29. *Daily Worker*, 10 August 1946.
30. Hinton, 'Self-help', p.107.
31. Hinton, 'Self-help and socialism', pp.107–10.
32. Jerzy Zubrzycki, *Polish Immigrants in Britain* (The Hague, 1956), pp.56ff.
33. *Bucks Advertiser*, 16 August 1946. The *News Chronicle* had already interviewed John Mann as the first squatter at the Vache.
34. *Daily Worker*, 10 August 1946. Interview with Maria Wylot, 13 May 2003
35. *Bucks Free Press*, 23 August 1946.
36. *Daily Worker*, 15 August 1946.
37. *Bucks Advertiser*, 23 August 1946.
38. *Bucks Examiner*, 16 and 23 August 1946.
39. Interview with June Parrymore, 21 April 2003.
40. *Bucks Free Press*, 23 August 1946; High Wycombe Housing Minutes, 7 September 1946 and 21 January 1947.

41. Jack Spector, 'Squatters: Occupation of Daws Hill Camp, High Wycombe', *OurHistory Journal*, 10, November 1985.
42. *Daily Worker*, 3 September 1946.
43. *Bucks Free Press*, 21 March 1947. I can however find no evidence that Jack Spector had been elected to West Wycombe parish council 'against Labour and Conservative opposition' (Spector, *Squatters*). His candidacy for Wycombe rural district council in March 1946 was promoted with the slogan 'Vote Spector for Progress' and with no mention of the communist party. (*Bucks Free Press*, 1 March 1946).
44. Interview with June Parrymore, 14 March 2003.
45. Interview with June Parrymore, 21 April 2003.
46. Wally Wright in personal conversation.
47. *Bucks Free Press*, 11 March 1966.
48. Wally was a widower and Flo a divorcee: interview with Joyce Hadfield, 11 April 2003.
49. Interview with Joyce Hadfield, 11 April 2003.
50. Letter from Arthur Slight, 29 March 2003.
51. Interview with Ernest Barnett, 22 April 2003.
52. Interview with June Parrymore, 14 March 2003; letters from Arthur Slight, 29 March 2003 and John Slight, 4 April 2003.
53. Interview with June Parrymore, 14 March 2003.
54. Interview with June Parrymore, 14 March 2003; Jack Spector, *Squatters*.
55. Interviews with Brenda Barnett, 22 April 2003 and Joyce Hadfield, 11 April 2003.
56. Interviews with Brenda Barnett, 22 April 2003 and Wyn Hawes, 23 March 2003.
57. Hinton, 'Self-help and socialism', pp.112–13.
58. *Information for Speakers*, 7 August 1946 (CPGB archives, National Museum of Labour History). Therefore a report of a public meeting on housing held by Amersham Communist Party could be headlined 'Government defended.' *Bucks Free Press*, 27 September 1946.
59. Ministry of Health, 18 September 1946, no.6. London Trades Council file, TUC Archive, HD 7333.
60. *Tribune*, 13 September 1946.
61. Harrington and Young, pp.62–63.
62. Hinton, 'Self-help and socialism', p.126.
63. Harry Pollitt file, CPGB archives.
64. *Bucks Examiner*, 23 August 1946.
65. Amersham RDC Minutes.
66. There were also asbestos huts at Chairborough Road in High Wycombe; interview with Ann Wilson, 22 April 2003.
67. David James, 'The Magic of Living' (http://members. iinet.au/~dcjames /story/html), ch. 2; Elizabeth Barry, 'Life as a Squatter' (work in progress)
68. Interview with Margaret Ward, 21 March 2003.
69. *Bucks Advertiser*, 27 June 1947.

70. ARDC Open Spaces Committee, 11 January 1949.
71. *Bucks Examiner*, 8 August 1947.
72. See Amersham RDC housing committee 16 September 1947.
73. Letter from Daisy Hunt, 22 March 2003.
74. *Bucks Examiner*, 28 January 1949.
75. *Bucks Examiner*, 4, 11 and 25 February 1949, Amersham RDC development committee 17 May 1949.
76. E mail from Elizabeth Barry, 31 March 2003.
77. Against 28 per cent for Labour, with the remainder split between other candidates. A bewildering eighteen candidates contested the eight seats in this ward. *Bucks Examiner*, 11 and 18 February 1949.
78. Amersham RDC housing manager's report, 14 March 1950.
79. Amersham RDC housing committee 20 May 1947 and rent and rates sub-committee 13 June 147.
80. *Bucks Free Press*, 27 March 1953.
81. Amersham RDC housing report, 17 May 1955.
82. Amersham RDC Hodgemoor Camp committee, 15 February 1956; treasurer's reports to Amersham RDC housing committee, 11 January and 6 December 1962.
83. Amersham RDC, report of the clerk to the council, 15 March 1956.
84. Amersham RDC, report of the clerk to the council, 15 May 1956.
85. Lorna Flint, *Wycombe Abbey School 1896–1986: A Partial History* (High Wycombe, 1989), pp.123–4, 130; High Wycombe borough council housing committee minutes, 17 September 1946.
86. Interview with David Williams, 3 April 2003.
87. Interview with Pamela Goodwin, 6 April 2003.
88. E mail from Trevor Fowler, 13 February 2003.
89. *Bucks Free Press*, 24 January 1947.
90. Interview with Wyn Hawes, 23 March 2003; borough council housing committee minutes.
91. Personal conversations.
92. *Bucks Free Press*, 8 November 1946. This was an election for two council seats, also contested by two Independent candidates.
93. Interview with John Burnham, 13 June 2002.
94. *Bucks Free Press*, 6 December 1946.
95. Spector, *Squatters*.
96. Interview with Ernest and Brenda Barnett, 22 April 2003.
97. Interview with Joyce Hadfield, 11 April 2003.
98. Interview with Wyn Hawes, 23 March 2003.
99. Interview with Ernest and Brenda Barnett, 22 April 2003.
100. Mark Ostrowski, 'History of the Polish Armed Forces 1939–49' (unpublished PhD at www.angelfire.com/ok2/polisharmy/chapter6.html, p.7); *Hansard*, vol. 447, cols 1332–3.
101. Wycombe Trades Union Council minutes.

102. AEU High Wycombe branch minutes, 10 February and 16 June 1949.
103. Zubrzycki, pp 83–85.
104. AEU High Wycombe No 2 branch minutes, 2 June 1949.
105. The general unions and some Labour MPs were more supportive of the Polish presence; see Zubrzycki, p.102.
106. Interview with June Parrymore, 21 April 2003.
107. *Bucks Examiner*, 16 April 1950.
108. Interview with Edna Burnham, 13 June 2002.
109. James, 'The magic'.
110. David Hans Gantzel, *Hazlemere* (High Wycombe, 1988), pp.162–3.
111. Interview with Stella Downes, 19 April 2003.
112. Interview with Marian and Maria Wylot, 13 May 2003.
113. Interview with Marian Wylot, 13 May 2003.
114. Interview with Marian and Maria Wylot, 13 May 2003.
115. Andrew Friend, *The Post War Squatters* in Nick Wates and Christian Wolmar, *Squatting: The Real Story* (London, 1980), p.14.
116. *Bucks Free Press*, 24 April 1953 and 4 April 1955.
117. Interview with Trevor Fowler, 23 April 2003.
118. Squatting is a civil offence in England, though a criminal offence in Scotland.
119. See for example Richard Croucher, *Engineers at War 1935–1945* (London, 1982), pp.213–14.
120. Speech at Leicester Square, 12 September 1946 (CPGB archives).
121. E.g. Hinton, 'Self-help and socialism', p.199, and thanks to David Renton for arguing this to provoke discussion.
122. Croucher, *Engineers at War*, p.373.
123. Martin Upham, 'The History of British Trotskyism to 1949' (Hull PhD, 1980).
124. Timmins, pp.140–150, Addison, p.58.
125. Noreen Branson, *History of the Communist Party of Great Britain 1941–51* (London, 1997), p.206.
126. Interview with Trevor Fowler, 23 April 2003.
127. Interview with Trevor Fowler.
128. Timmins, pp.179–192.
129. Amersham RDC Minutes, 22 February 1949.
130. L. J. Mayes, *The History of the Borough of High Wycombe from 1880 to the Present Day* (London, 1960) pp.85–6; interview with Alan and June Parrymore, 21 April 2003.
131. Renie Lester from Scunthorpe, quoted in Addison, *Now the War Is Over*, p.67.
132. (Bucks Federation of Women's Institutes), *Squatting at the Vache* (Newbury, 1993), pp.219–21.
133. Interview with Joyce Hadfield, 11 April 2003.
134. Interview with Margaret Ward, 21 March 2003.
135. Ward, 'Direct action for houses', p.13.
136. Paul Balchin, *Housing Policy: An introduction* (London, 1995), p.6.

Agency and Ethnicity
A pamphlet by the East London (Jewish) Branch of the Social Democratic Federation

David Young

The historiography of the Social Democratic Federation (SDF) is haunted by ghosts. These spectres reveal themselves in the myths of racism, sexism, elitism and sectarianism that surround the SDF. Their advocacy of marxian socialism has led them to be described as 'alien' and un-British, while their criticisms of the Labour Party and trade unions gained them the label of 'dogmatic' and 'sectarian'. The actions of H.M. Hyndman, the SDF's leading personality, who preached revolution but was also a stockbroker has lent credence to their image as a group of cranks and outsiders.[1] As David Howell has remarked, however, this 'image of the Social Democratic Federation…is a tendentious, partial and misleading one…Clearly the reality was more complex than this.'[2]

In this article I intend to explore one aspect of this image—the relationship between the SDF and Jews—and indulge in a little ghostbusting by focusing on the contents of a Yiddish pamphlet that, to the best of my knowledge, has not previously been referred to in work on the SDF. In particular, I aim to show that, contrary to the prevailing image of the SDF, the pamphlet represents a positive role for its Jewish members in the SDF and an active engagement with the Jewish working class of London's East End. I will also contrast the language used in this text with that used in similar works by more prominent SDFers such as Harry Quelch and Ernest Belfort Bax to illustrate the different interpretations put on the same policies by groups within the SDF and between semi-autonomous branches and the centre.

The SDF, Jews and anti-semitism

In an article published in 1952 Edmund Silberner notes that 'none of the British Social Democrats seem to have liked the Jews.'[3] This bold statement has been followed over the past half century by frequent references to the anti-semitism of the SDF. For example, in *The Jewish Immigrant in England* published in 1960, Lloyd P. Gartner developed this line of argument. Citing Silberner in support Gartner wrote that the SDF was:

> not neutral but negative towards the Jews, Hyndman who dominated English Marxists absolutely, was an anti-Semite and the Federation's journal *Justice* amply expressed these views. Although the anti-Semitism of these English Marxists was ostensibly aimed only at Jewish capitalists, it bore enough animus to extend to Jews without capital and at times, to fellow Marxists who happened to be Jewish.[4]

Hyndman therefore seems to be the most obvious culprit amongst the leadership. In 1961 his biographer Tsuzuki described him as 'causing much offence' even though during this period 'anti-Semitism was not uncommon in left-wing circles.' For example, in the wake of the Jameson Raid Hyndman claimed that the Boers were 'less criminal' than the 'Jewish financiers' who had funded the expedition and three years later when hostilities broke out he continually referred to the conflict in South Africa as the 'Jew's war' while the press became the 'Jew jingo press'.[5]

Making spurious connections between Jews, finance-capital and anti-semitism in general was not uncommon among figures in public life at this time.[6] Moreover, despite Gartner's claim, Hyndman is not solely to blame for the SDF's reputation. The party newspaper *Justice*, in the hands of its editor Harry Quelch, issued forth a series of anti-semitic statements and opinions. *Justice* frequently described Jews in stereotypical terms followed by a denial that the writer believed this. For example, the *Justice* of the 28 August 1899 stated that 'We do not aver that the Jews have themselves to thank to a great extent for the bitter feeling against them…They are exceedingly purse-proud when wealthy, very arrogant, very unscrupulous and very clannish.'[7]

In a more recent work Jonathan Schneer writes of the SDF that 'an ugly strain of racism and anti-Semitism was always present in London's premier socialist body. Scholars who have neglected or minimised this aspect of its history have provided less than a full and realistic picture of the organisation.'[8] Although it is not clear which scholars he is referring to, Hyndman, *Justice* and the SDF seem to be synonymous in the literature with anti-semitism. Nevertheless, as Schneer also points out, the racist pronouncements of Hyndman and others did not go unanswered within the SDF. Indeed, in comparing the SDF's anti-semitism and its attitudes to feminism and women's rights, Karen Hunt has shown that 'within the SDF anti-racist members were more successful in making their case than the anti-sexists'.[9]

Hence, when Hyndman blamed the outbreak of war in South Africa on 'the butchering Semites'[10] he came up against not only Theodore Rothstein and Belfort Bax but the readership of *Justice* and later the membership of the federation.

Rothstein objected to the anti-semitism put forward by Hyndman and demanded an executive resolution condemning what he later described as 'this indelible stain on English socialism.'[11] Bax criticised Hyndman's lack of socialist analysis as well as his anti-semitism. 'I am a pro-Boer', declared Bax, not because he was patriotic from the Boers' standpoint, but rather because he was resisting 'the violence of Great Britain and international capitalism'. Therefore, in Bax's view, what lay behind 'the attempt to throw the blame for the war on the Jews' was an accidental affection for one capitalist state over another. 'If there is one doctrine fundamental to Socialism', asserted Bax, 'it is of the class struggle superseding the national struggle'.[12]

These criticisms of Hyndman and the editorial line of *Justice* were reproduced in the correspondence columns of the newspaper. For example, M. Shayer, who later became a supporter of Zionism, wrote that *Justice* was 'on the high road to anti-Semitism…We accept your assurance of your good sentiments but *Justice* cannot be judged by that; it must be judged by what you write in it.' J. B. Askew, a more prominent SDFer and one who was active in the Second International, commented that he thought it was 'a serious question for the SDF how long they can with impunity allow their organ to be made a playground for certain members to air their fads in, and to endanger the whole cause of Social Democracy thereby'.[13]

This criticism led to a resolution being put forward at the 1900 annual conference of the SDF, where Dan Irving charged *Justice* with having contained anti-semitic articles. Usually Irving is seen as a staunch Hyndmanite member of the 'Old Guard', and it may not be coincidental that in April 1908 he had fought a by-election at North West Manchester where his supporters were 'mainly from the Jewish community'.[14] Harry Quelch as editor denied the charges against *Justice*, but Joseph Finn—described in the conference report as a 'Jewish comrade'—declared that the articles 'might be construed as raising race hatred', while John Spargo said that they created 'an anti-Semitic feeling by such phrases as "a gang of Jew capitalists".' Demonstrating just what they had been complaining about, Quelch in his reply claimed that if:

> certain capitalists Jews for their own purposes, tried to make out what had been said in *Justice* was anti-Semitic, he could not help it. The war was being held up to people as an object for patriotism. They had explained

that the war was being carried out in the interests of an international financial gang, most of whom were Jews. They had said nothing against the capitalist Jew that they were not prepared to say against the British capitalist, but apparently if a man was a Jew nothing must be said against him.[15]

Nevertheless, the resolution was passed regretting that 'any impression should have gained ground that *Justice*, by its articles, or the SDF generally, is in any way anti-Semitic' and stating its opposition to 'all anti-Semitic parties and national antagonisms without distinction of race and creed.' Although the resolution did not eliminate anti-semitism from British socialism it did go some way to quelling the voicing of the anti-semitic opinions of Hyndman and others.[16] If nothing else, it shows the debate occurring *within* the SDF on nationalism, racism and anti-semitism, and it is significant that many of the most active participants in the debate were Jewish members of the federation.

Jewish organisation within the SDF

The SDF and the Socialist League had active contacts with the Jewish population in East London from the mid-1880s. William Fishman points out that while the Socialist League seemed more sympathetic to the local population, the SDF provided support for those arrested after a raid on the Berner Street club in March 1889 and for a strike of Jewish tailors led by William Weiss in September and October 1889.[17] As early as 1885, Justice had claimed that 'the success of the movement amongst the Jews in East London has already been quite remarkable. Thousands of them, we speak without any exaggeration whatever, have already taken up with the doctrines of Socialism in a greater or less degree.' But, as Fishman points out, it would be perhaps twenty years before this statement would be valid.[18]

By the turn of the century the influx of Jewish immigrants into the East End of London had certainly provided a fertile ground for marxist socialism, as well as a breeding ground for racist and anti-semitic opposition. Between fifty and sixty thousand Jews entered the country between 1890 and 1902, while the total Jewish population for London in 1903 has been given as between 140,000 and 150,000.[19] These immigrants were concentrated in particular parts of the city. For example, the 'alien' population of Whitechapel went up from 24.1 per cent to 31.8 per cent between 1891 and 1901 while that of St Georges in the East went up from 16.2 per cent to 28.8 per cent and Mile End Old Town more than doubled from 5.3 per cent to 11.5 per cent in the same period.[20] In employment terms these immigrants were heavily concentrated in tailoring and boot and shoe manufacture. In 1880 these trades represented over 37 per cent of Jews employed in the East End while by 1901 it was nearly 58 per cent.[21] The politics of the East End of this period were largely formed by race. Even the Jewish MPs and the Jewish relief organisations for the area supported restrictions on alien immigration, and SDF candidates and other labour figures opposed 'Chinese slavery'.[22] It was into this sort of community that the East London (Jewish) branch was born in the early 1900s.

From the 1870s there were Jewish socialist and radical organisations in the community in the East End which published newspapers in Yiddish,[23] while the anarchist journal the *Arbeiter Fraint* (Workers' Friend) was published in London from 1885 but was also well known in Russia.[24] However, the Jewish Socialist party Poale Zion was reported as 'very weak' with members 'numbered in tens rather than hundreds.'[25] According to Walter Kendall, from the 1880s for many Russian and Jewish Russian socialists 'the marxist character of the SDF proved it to be their natural home.'[26] This is a point also put forward by Paul Thompson when he states that the 'instinct for doctrine' amongst Jewish social democrats made them influential members 'winning many branches to a more clearly Marxist and internationalist standpoint.'[27] In 1893 and 1894 notices in Justice told readers of a new SDF branch formed in Whitechapel 'mainly composed of our *Jewish* comrades from the old Christian-street Club' where

> can be seen various Socialist periodicals in the Hebrew language, printed in America. They also have Hebrew translations of Lassalle's 'Working Man's Programme', Bebel's great speech in the Reichstag, and other pamphlets. Any comrades who can speak in German or Yiddish, or both, will be heartily welcomed at the meetings.[28]

The East London (Jewish) branch of the SDF is mentioned as sending a delegate to the annual conference between 1903 and 1907 and as with other branches may have had a relatively short life as it is last mentioned in the directory of *Justice* in the edition of 24 August 1907. There was also a West London (Jewish) branch which had a brief existence in 1907 based in Soho.[29] The SDF provided a link between British socialism and the Jewish community and between British socialism and Russian Jewish socialism. This link between Russia and Britain was exemplified when on 21 March 1903 Lenin was advertised as taking part in a large meeting of the East London (Jewish) branch.[30] Joseph Finn, a leading member of the East London (Jewish) branch, was able to set up the 'relatively strong' United Ladies' Tailors' and Mantle Makers' Union.[31] The East London (Jewish) branch also had links with the Bund: at a meeting to protest against the Kishinev massacres on 21 June 1903 the SDF delegates called initially for a ban on Zionists at the meeting and secondly to support the Bund in Russia and Poland. The rejection of the resolution subsequently caused divisions within the local Jewish labour movement.[32] Nira Yuval-Davis describes the Bund as 'vehemently anti-Zionist' and the East London (Jewish) branch of the SDF seem to have adopted a similar set of policies.[33] The Bundist idea of an autonomous socialist organisation which could fight against anti-semitism while, at the same time, promoting class struggle amongst Jews in a Jewish language within a socialist federation sits easily with the formation of Jewish branches and the affiliation of the London branch of the Polish socialist party within the SDF.[34] In 1904 the branch organised a demonstration against immigration controls. For Steve Cohen the SDF's response was 'to put it mildly, fainthearted' and he cites Hyndman as speaking to the meeting declaring that 'he was against "free admittance of all aliens" and going on to attack Jews for living in ghettos and refusing to intermarry.'[35]

Apart from Finn, whom we saw criticising *Justice* at the 1900 SDF conference, other names associated with the East London (Jewish) branch include S. Schwartz, who was the branch delegate to the SDF conferences in 1906 and 1907, and Boris Kahan, who was recorded as the branch secretary in 1907 and was a delegate to the conference each year between 1903 and 1906. Elia Levin—an observer to the Russian Social Democratic and Labour Party conference in 1907—was branch secretary before transferring to the Whitechapel branch later in 1907.[36] Boris Kahan and his sister Zelda were prominent voices in the internationalist opposition to Hyndman in the years before the First World War. At the 1903 conference he successfully proposed a motion condemning the current anti-alien legislation and calling for the right to asylum, arguing that Britain itself was 'one of the great emigrating countries' and should not put up its own barriers.[37]

What is Social Democracy?

Published in March 1902, the pamphlet *What is Social Democracy?* is the most substantial surviving document of this period of activity by the East London (Jewish) branch. Thirty-two pages long and hence a 'double-strength' pamphlet, it is written entirely in 'Western' Yiddish, although occasionally some specifically English words like 'rates' are rendered in English using Hebrew characters.[38] The pamphlet was published at what it described as a 'critical time' in the activity of the branch, coinciding with the war in South Africa, the prospect of conscription and the recent Taff Vale judgement against the trade unions. The 'English population', it claimed, had been 'overcome by chauvinism…in agreement with the general reactionary forces' while the Jewish worker was 'soaked with bourgeois ideas without understanding the elementary interests of his class. He is dragged by the Zionist movement and its bourgeois ideas.' With anti-semitism increasing outside of the Jewish community and the 'grossest ignorance of class interests' prevailing within it, the pamphlet issued its rallying call: 'It is the duty of each Social Democrat to join the Jewish branch and together with us under the united flag of the English Social Democrats to work amongst the Jewish masses to implement our socialist ideas.'

The introduction to the pamphlet is of interest as describing the aims and objectives of the branch. Stating that the Jewish branch had been set up mainly for 'tactical' reasons, it insisted that, like all of its 'sister' branches, it stood on a platform of international socialism recognising only the distinction 'between classes and not races or nations'. Because of the specific needs of Jewish workers in terms of language and conditions, and because the 'English branch' did not want to be connected with these problems, the branch had decided to organise itself separately. Nevertheless, it fought not only against the 'chauvinist currents' of imperialism, anti-semitism, but also against Zionism. 'Both these extremes are for the branch offspring of the same bourgeois seed and both can blind the worker and lead him astray from the direct route to liberation. In every country the branch wants to see Jewish workers as citizens and therefore it considers the struggle for citizens' rights one of its most important duties.'

Describing what it saw as the ever-increasing pace of the class struggle, the pamphlet argued that the best way to assist in the development of this process was to 'take part mightily in the real life of the worker and not to stand aside as a critical observer and remain satisfied with theoretical conclusions…' As has now become increasingly widely recognised, this meant that the attitude adopted towards trade unions was far more complex than used to be associated with the SDF. Arguing that Jewish workers in London remained strongly influenced by petty-bourgeois ideas and largely ignorant of the 'basic questions of the class struggle', the pamphlet argued for serious and sustained work within the trade unions. 'Flirting with the ruling masters' foolish feelings of selfish competitiveness and "jealousy" of one union towards the other, ambitions of academics, petty-mindedness and egoism of individual trades, all this has to be got rid of.' On the other hand, the pamphlet also argued against 'so-called "pure-and-simple" trade unionism', urging that even within the unions the socialist 'must not ever forget that basic stance from which he must perceive the struggle'. The ideal, less sectarian than is sometimes imagined, was that both political and industrial forms of activity should be 'united'.

Most of the pamphlet comprises sections on the SDF's programme, its demands for 'transitional measures', both local and national, and for 'political reforms' of a democratic character such as Logie Barrow and Ian Bullock have described in their book *Democracy and the Labour Movement*.[39] In many ways these sections are typical of SDF publications of the period, and the sections on programme and transitional measures closely resemble the 1903 revised version of the SDF programme reproduced by R.C.K. Ensor in his book *Modern Socialism*.[40] However, there are also a number of differences that mark the pamphlet out as the product of a particular branch, notably in the order, and implicitly the priority, it gives the individual policies. For example, the Yiddish pamphlet stands the SDF programme on its head by listing education as the first of the 'transitional measures' and in the short list of the 'Aims'. The demand for free and secular education was a mainstay of radical and socialist policy from the mid-nineteenth century, and the emphasis on technical education was a focus of SDF policy from the end of the nineteenth century. At the same time as a section of the SDF were developing the concept of Independent Working Class Education that would take an institutional form with the Plebs League in 1909, the majority in the party were demanding 'useful' education in terms of industrial trade skills. Though the emphasis is slightly different, this demand still puts the Jewish branch very much in the mainstream of the party.[41]

More distinctively, the Yiddish pamphlet gives a significant amount of space to the issue of constitutional reform. Here it may be contrasted with similar SDF agitational pamphlets of the period, for example the Brixton branch's undated *What we want! An address to our neighbours*, which concentrates on municipal issues, and *An Address to the men and women of Bow and Bromley*, dating from about 1893, which again focuses on local issues—but without the emphasis on political reform.[42] This emphasis may be because the bulk of the pamphlet's intended readership will have been newly arrived from Poland, Russia and Germany and hence democratic measures and popular control of governments are likely to have caught their imagination. However, it is an indication of the continuities in the SDF's radicalism that political reforms should be placed on the same level as the economic essentials of the class struggle. Many of these demands, such as the payment of MPs, universal adult suffrage, proportional representation and the abolition of the monarchy, would not have seemed unfamiliar to the Chartists half a century before.

A related point of interest is the priority given to the referendum in the East London pamphlet. According to Barrow and Bullock, 'control of the elected, and active participation in decision-making through various means including the referendum, were essential features of what the SDF meant by Social Democracy'.[43] The referendum and the initiative were causes which the SDF had espoused from the 1880s. In 1884 Hyndman had mentioned the proposal for a National Convention and that 'no laws should be made…without reference to the vote of the entire people'.[44] In 1893 and again in 1900 the Socialist International had encouraged parties to agitate for the referendum and the initiative. Here it appears in two sections of the text, suggesting that it was a measure that would appeal to its Yiddish-speaking readership. Such emphases may also be contrasted with the nationalism of the Zionists, who believed democracy, outside of a Jewish state, to be bankrupt. Implicitly, by advancing these democratic demands, the Jewish socialists of the SDF were also arguing for their inclusion within the state.

It may also be significant that the one political demand which the Yiddish pamphlet omits from the list is that granting 'foreigners…rights of citizenship after two years' residence in the country, on the recommendation of four British-born citizens, without any fees'.[45] It is possible that the Jewish branch opposed this policy, or at least thought it may prove unpopular with the pamphlet's prospective readership. Alternatively, it may have been excluded to deflect possible opposition of the non-Jewish (and possibly anti-semitic) population of the East End. In this connection, an illuminating comparison can be made between the contents of this pamphlet and one published two years later by the SDF branch in nearby Canning Town. This pamphlet, *Chinese Slavery in the Transvaal and White Slavery and Poverty at Home*, was produced in support of Will Thorne's parliamentary election campaign and shows how fears of dilution by foreign workers were used as a means of attracting political support.[46] Though the pamphlet features a Crane-like drawing of an angel linking arms with workers, under a banner resplendent with 'The unity of labour is the hope of the world', the text itself leaves a rather different impression. Thus, Thorne's objections to Chinese workers on 'economic, moral and sanitary grounds' include their underselling of the white labourer and living on food which 'would spell death to a man of European birth'. The 'Chinaman', the pamphlet states in no uncertain terms, brought 'certain nameless vices into his new domicile, and an indigent white population apprehends with an agony of suspicion and horror the possible corruption of its children by the yellow invader'. An SDF member since 1886 who was to be elected to parliament in 1906, Thorne used this as an argument for the payment of a decent wage to 'English workmen', rather than resorting to immigrant labour. The fact that these two publications could be produced almost side by side confirms that the executive of the SDF allowed its branches a significant degree of local autonomy.

One area of policy that does not appear in any other SDF publication is anti-Zionism. At two points in the text, the Yiddish pamphlet criticises the 'petty-bourgeois' nature of Zionism and groups it with anti-semitism and imperialism as an obstacle to the liberation of the Jewish worker. If this suggests that already the Zionist movement was influential enough to act as a drag on socialist activity among London Jews, it also confirms that the Jewish branch was closer to the Bundists than the Zionists or Jewish nationalists and did not advocate separate Jewish organisation as a matter of fundamental principle.

Agency and determinism

Comparing the pamphlet with contemporaneous productions like Harry Quelch's *Economics of Labour* and *A New Catechism of Socialism* by Quelch and Ernest Belfort Bax, one of the most distinctive features of the Yiddish text is the emphasis it gives to experience and collective agency in the achievement of socialism. In describing their work, the authors briefly appear to espouse a form of economic determinism in presenting socialism as 'the necessary result of the development of present society. A result which is formed every day and every moment, and is surer by the engine of economic progress.'[47] However, the pamphlet also describes how the development of capitalism 'calls for the emergence of its own means of rectification', and it is this implicit focus on the action inherent in class consciousness that marks the pamphlet out from 'standard' SDF texts.

In a long section describing the development of class consciousness the word 'struggle' is used constantly—fourteen times over two pages. Class consciousness is acquired through everyday experience or as they phrase it—perhaps in reference to the SDF's own theoreticians—as 'a product of real life and not a mere theoretical construct of some philosopher'. Rising up in 'united struggle against the enemy', the working class is depicted in martial terms.

In this struggle, in the storm and passion of industrial battles, the class consciousness, the consciousness of the basic antagonism of the working class and ruling class and the consciousness of the necessity to get organised in a sharply divided class party, this class consciousness is established and grows in the worker, first slowly but later faster and faster. Thus the struggle becomes a class struggle and the proletariat becomes a fanatical carrier of the socialist idea.

This sense of class consciousness as being 'borne in the storm and passion of everyday life' also informs the pamphlet's view of political tactics, which towards the end of the introduction are summarised as follows: 'the struggle must be carried out bravely, ambitiously, and properly and the consciousness of the fact that the worker is nothing more than a part of the general class struggle leading to the elimination of private property and the implementing of the socialist ideal which is taking place between the exploiters and the exploited on all fronts, among all nations, must be present.'

This type of language differs from that used in other SDF publications in its emphasis on struggle, experience, agency and action rather than economic determinism, the evolution of capitalism and the inevitability of socialism. For example, in the *New Catechism of Socialism* Bax and Quelch begin by describing socialism as the common ownership of the means of production followed by brief restatements of marxian economics, with a focus on surplus value, and the materialist conception of history. The emphasis is on evolution rather than agency and action. When later in the work the class struggle is brought into play, it is almost as its by-product rather than its motive-force.[48] Harry Quelch had direct experience of the hopes and passions of the class struggle as an organiser of the South Side Protection League during the dock strike of 1889. Despite this experience, there is a feeling of inevitability about his exposition of marxist economics. In his *Economics of Labour* he describes 'the inexorable working of…economic laws' and states that 'the proletarian is necessary to capitalism, and thus capitalism produces the proletarian which is necessary for its existence'.[49] Although he criticises temperance, thrift and free trade as chimeras for the working class there is no advocacy of raising class consciousness and advancing the class struggle as in the Yiddish pamphlet.

In 1917, in the wake of the Tsar's abdication, Sam Farrow addressed the delegates at the BSP's annual conference which he was chairing. He described the party's task at this time of war weariness and discontent as 'to educate the workers so that when the hour of Social Revolution strikes, they will have the necessary training and discipline to accomplish their emancipation'.[50] Hence, there was no conception of leading the class struggle or of 'the revolution' as something to be planned or directed by a socialist party. This attitude to class struggle and revolutionary activity can be traced back through the rhetoric of most mainstream SDF publications. A.P. Hazell, a leading SDFer from North London called on workers to 'Recognise your servitude!' and to 'Study history and see how you have been robbed through the ages.' His strategy was for workers to 'appoint [their] own administrators and establish a Socialist Commonwealth in which your poverty can have no place…'[51] Hazell's view was that workers needed to acknowledge their exploitation and elect socialists to implement the new society. B. O'Donnell, in a pamphlet published soon after *What is Social Democracy?*, wrote:

> Well, my friends, the remedy lies in your hands. By the very fact of your numbers you control completely the ballot-box at election times…If I have convinced you that the present system is iniquitous and harmful then your only course is to fight for Socialism and the substitution of co-operative, in place of competitive, action.[52]

James Leatham, another prolific SDF writer, published *The Class War: A Lecture* which went into many editions. However, despite the inflammatory title he announced that 'we don't preach hatred of men, but hatred of systems and of men's characters which are the outcome of the false and bad in these systems'. The working class 'must read and listen, and then [they] will know how ignorant [they] are'—and thus, he hoped, move towards electing socialist representatives.[53] A last example from 1894 illustrates the same thread of rhetoric as the BSP activist a generation later. D. Campbell tells his readers that 'We know we must wait! Wait and work continuously until the slow creeping hour arrives, when [the working class] will realise the full import of the message in mind and heart.'[54] Though only a few illustrative cases can be presented here, the tone of these mainstream texts is very different from the emphasis on experience and collective agency to be found in the Yiddish pamphlet.

Reflections

The character of such publications can tell us a lot about the relationship between the SDF and its members. Unfortunately, there is no central archive of SDF material nor any substantial bibliography of SDF publications at a national level, let alone its local newspapers and other publications. However, the evidence of this particular text suggests that, at least in respect of the relationship between the SDF and its Jewish members, a wider reappraisal may be necessary. First, it is necessary to reassess the view that the SDF was an anti-semitic and racist organisation. Although anti-semitic statements appeared in *Justice*, they did not go unanswered and the culture of the SDF did not stop Jews from becoming members of its national executive. Indeed, *What is Social Democracy?* shows how Jewish members were able to establish their own separate organisation *within* the SDF. While some women saw this as an ideal for women socialists in the SDF, this was not possible as members of the Women's Circles were not integrated fully into the membership until 1909.[55] Jewish members in East London, on the other hand, had their own branch, managed to issue a short series of publications and, in *Di Naye Velt*, their own newspaper. This suggests that in this respect at least the SDF operated more as a federation which was readier to accommodate local conditions than the rigid organisation of legend would suggest. It is true that the pamphlet reaffirms the bulk of the SDF programme which was itself consistent with the mainstream of European socialism with which many members of the branch may already have been familiar. Nevertheless, the scope for different emphases may clearly be seen both in the pamphlet's anti-Zionism and its appeal to democratic reforms couched in a class-struggle rhetoric.

I would like to acknowledge the helpful advice and comments made by Kevin Morgan, Andrew MacMullen, Graham Horry and an anonymous referee on earlier versions of this essay.

Notes

1. See Henry Pelling, *The Origins of the Labour Party* (Oxford, 1965). For discussions of images of the SDF, see Karen Hunt, *Equivocal Feminists. The Social Democratic Federation and the woman question 1884–1911* (Cambridge, 1996) pp.7–16 and Martin Crick, *The History of the Social Democratic Federation* (Keele, 1994).
2. David Howell, *British Workers and the Independent Labour Party 1888–1906* (Manchester, 1983), p.389.
3. Edmund Silberner, 'British socialism and the Jews', *Historica Judaica* (April 1952), p.39.
4. Lloyd P. Gartner, *The Jewish Immigrant in England 1970–1914* (London, 1960), p.127.
5. Chushichi Tsuzuki, *H. M. Hyndman and British Socialism* (Oxford, 1961), pp.126, 128. See *Justice*, 7 October 1899 for 'The Jews' war on the Transvaal'. See also Norman Etherington, 'Hyndman, the Social Democratic Federation and imperialism', *Historical Studies*, 16 (1974), p. 99, Bill Baker, *The Social Democratic Federation and the Boer War* (London, 1974) pp.5–6; Paul Ward, *Red Flag and Union Jack, Englishness, Patriotism and the British Left, 1881–1924* (Woodbridge 1998); pp.68–75.
6. See for example Claire Hirschfield, 'The Anglo-Boer War and the issue of Jewish culpability', *Journal of Contemporary History*, 15, 4 (1980).
7. Cited Hunt, *Equivocal Feminists*, p.73. See also Baker, *SDF and the Boer War*, citing an article by 'Sandy MacFarlane' on the Dreyfus affair.
8. Jonathan Schneer, *London 1900: The Imperial Metropolis* (New Haven, 1999), p.170.
9. Hunt, *Equivocal Feminists*, pp.70–7.
10. *Justice*, 11 July 1899.

11. *Justice*, 21 and 28 October 1899.
12. *Justice*, 28 October 1899.
13. Cited Hunt, *Equivocal Feminists*, pp.72–3. Shayer had been the Whitechapel branch delegate to the congress of the Second International in London in 1896.
14. See Lawrence Chew, 'Dan Irving and Socialist Politics in Burnley 1880–1924', *North West Labour History*, 23 (1998–9), p.8.
15. SDF annual conference *Report*, 1900, p.18.
16. See Schneer, *London 1900*, p.170, Hunt, *Equivocal Feminists* p.74, and Baker, *SDF and the Boer War*, p.6.
17. William Fishman, *East End Jewish Radicals* (London, 1975) pp.168, 176.
18. Fishman, *East End Jewish Radicals*, pp.150–1.
19. V.D. Lipman, *The Social History of the Jews in England 1850–1950* (London, 1954), pp.88, 99. See also David Feldman, 'The importance of being English. Jewish immigration and the decay of liberal England' in David Feldman and Gareth Stedman Jones (eds), *Metropolis London: Histories and Representations since 1800* (London, 1989), pp.56–7.
20. Lipman, *Jews in England*, pp.94–5.
21. Lipman, *Jews in England*, pp.106–7.
22. See Henry Pelling, *Social Geography of British Elections 1885–1910* (London, 1968) pp.42–8, Feldman, 'Importance', pp.62–6.
23. Lipman, *Jews in England*, pp.131–2, Fishman, *East End Jewish Radicals*.
24. Lipman, *Jews in England*, pp.132–3, Walter Kendall, 'Russian emigration and British Marxist Socialism', *International Review of Social History* (1963), pp.352–3.
25. Geoffrey Alderman, 'The political impact of Zionism in the East End of London before 1940', *London Journal*, 9, 1 (1983), p.35.
26. Kendall, 'Russian emigration'., p.353.
27. Paul Thompson, *Socialists, Liberals and Labour. The struggle for London 1885–1914* (London, 1967) p.31.
28. *Justice*, 9 December 1893, 24 March 1894.
29. SDF annual conference *Reports*, 1903–7, *Justice*, 8 June and 24 August 1907, For four years the delegate was Boris Kahan. Kahan was born in Kiev in 1877 and was the brother of Zelda Kahan; see Walter Kendall, *The Revolutionary Movement in Britain 1900–1921* (London, 1969) p.332.
30. Tish Collins, 'Lenin, *Iskra* and Clerkenwell', *Bulletin of the Marx Memorial Library*, 135 (2002).
31. Paul Thompson, *Socialists, Liberals and Labour*. p.31, Gartner, *Jewish immigrant*, p.137.
32. Rudolf Rocker claims that this was especially divisive because the Zionists were 'a negligible factor among the Jewish workers in London'. Rudolf Rocker, *The London Years* (London, 1956), pp.137, 162–3.
33. Nira Yuval-Davis, 'Marxism and Jewish Nationalism', *History Workshop Journal*, 24 (1987), p.92.
34. For the Polish Socialist party in London see SDF annual conference *Report* 1904. The London branch of the Bund was in contact with the Stratford branch of

the SDF: see Stratford SDF Minutes, 25 April 1907.
35. Steve Cohen, *That's Funny, You Don't Look Anti-Semitic. An anti-racist analysis of left anti-semitism* (Leeds, 1984), p.22.
36. *Justice*, 30 March 1907. Levin is mentioned as branch secretary in the Stratford SDF minutes for this period. Boris Kahan attended the 1906 Bradford conference as the delegate for the Mile End branch. This degree of fluidity in the representation of branches was not unusual.
37. SDF annual conference *Report*, 1903, p.24.
38. I would like to acknowledge the work of Dr Rudolf Uvira, Palacky University, Olomouc, Czech Republic and Jitka Young in the translation of the text of the pamphlet.
39. Logie Barrow and Ian Bullock, *Democratic Ideas and the British Labour Movement 1880–1914* (Cambridge, 1996).
40. R.C.K. Ensor, *Modern Socialism* (London, 1904), pp.350–5.
41. On child maintenance see, J. Hunter Watts, *State Maintenance for Children* (London, 1904); for technical education see Countess of Warwick, *A Nation's Youth. Physical deterioration: its cause and some remedies* (London, 1906); and on the education debate generally see Hilda Kean, *Challenging the State: the socialist and feminist educational experience 1900–1930* (London, 1990). At the 1907 Labour Party conference Will Thorne ('the SDF MP') proposed and carried a resolution for free secular, technical state education.
42. For other publications in a similar vein, see the SDF/Social Democratic Party pamphlets *An Appeal to the workers of Camberwell* (London, n.d.) and *To the Electors of Deptford* (London, 1898).
43. Barrow and Bullock, *Democratic Ideas*, p.17.
44. *Justice*, 14 June 1884 cited Barrow and Bullock, *Democratic Ideas*, p.15. See also Hyndman, *England For All* (London, 1881), pp.88–111.
45. Ensor, *Modern Socialism*, p.353.
46. Will Thorne, *Chinese Slavery in the Transvaal and White Slavery and Poverty at Home* (London, n.d. but 1904).
47. Following references all from *What is Social Democracy?*, pp.5–7.
48. Ernest Belfort Bax and Harry Quelch, *A New Catechism of Socialism* (1909; first published 1900), pp.7–29. Bax's emphasis on history and the evolution of human society is evident in his other co-authored work: William Morris and Ernest Belfort Bax, *Socialism: Its Growth and Outcome* (London, 1893).
49. Harry Quelch, *The Economics of Labour* (London, n.d.), p.14.
50. Cited Kendall, *Revolutionary Movement*, p.173.
51. A.P. Hazell, *Slavedom, Serfdom and Wagedom* (London, 1910), p.15.
52. B. O'Donnell, *The Evils of Competition* (London, 1904), p.15.
53. James Leatham, *The Class War: A Lecture* (London, 1916 edn), p.11.
54. D. Campbell, *The Unemployed Problem: the socialist solution* (London, 1894), p.13.
55. Karen Hunt, *Equivocal Feminists*, pp.236–7.

Edward Terrill and the Fifth Monarchy

Charles Hobday

The *Records of a Church of Christ*, a history of Broadmead Baptist Church in Bristol from 1640 to 1687, is an invaluable source of information on the inner life of a Dissenting congregation under the Restoration.[1] Nearly three-quarters of the book, covering the period up to 1679, is the work of Edward Terrill, the remainder being added by other members of the church. Almost all aspects of its organisation and activities are covered and the accounts of the persecution which its members periodically suffered are dramatic and often moving. Yet a dimension is missing: the political. Throughout the Restoration period Bristol—a 'most factious city...worse than Taunton', Judge Jeffreys called it [2]—was a centre of anti-government intrigue, in which Dissenters took the lead; yet the authors of the *Records*, who did not know into whose hands the manuscript might fall, give no indication the members of the church were involved in politics. However, a careful reading of the *Records* in conjunction with other documents suggests that under Terrill's leadership Broadmead adopted a radical and even revolutionary ideology.

Thrift and the millennium

Terrill, the son of a farmer, was born at Almondsbury in Gloucestershire in 1634, and was apprenticed to a Bristol scrivener. After his indentures expired he combined practice as a scrivener with running a school, and in 1660 was admitted a freeman of Bristol. By 1654 he had become a follower of Thomas Ewins, the spiritual guide of the group which was to develop into the Broadmead church, and in 1658 he was baptised and admitted to church membership. Through Broadmead he met Thomas Ellis, a merchant who in 1662 was elected one of its two ruling elders. Ellis in 1665 established a sugar refinery, and shortly afterwards Terrill entered into partnership with him. When Ellis retired from the business Terrill bought up his share, and at his death he was rich enough to bequeath considerable property in land and houses to the church.³

He was elected an elder in 1667, and in this capacity proved a strict disciplinarian. Of the six occasions after his election when members were expelled from the church, one occurred when it had no pastor and three when the pastor was in London, so that responsibility for discipline devolved upon the elders. Three men were expelled for drunkenness, another for not attending services, and a widow for borrowing money and failing to repay it. A servant girl who was found to be pregnant by her employer was also expelled, although Terrill succeeded in persuading him to marry her.⁴

So far he fits into the conventional picture of the Dissenters of the Restoration period, abandoning their revolutionary dreams to devote themselves to the development of industry and commerce, and enforcing the Protestant ethic of temperance, chastity, thrift, hard work and honest dealing There was another side to him, however, for there is strong evidence that he shared the millenarian hopes of the Fifth Monarchy Men, and possibly their readiness to use force to establish the Rule of the Saints.

It is not always easy to decide who should or should not be described as a Fifth Monarchist, for millenarian ideas were widely accepted among Protestants. That the Papacy and the Empire, the heirs of the Roman Empire, were the fourth of the monarchies described in *Daniel vii*; that the Papacy was also the Babylon denounced in *Revelation xvii–xviii*; that their destruction was imminent, and would be followed by the Fifth Monarchy of Christ and his Saints, who would rule for a thousand years—all these ideas were commonplaces. The Fifth Monarchists shared with other radicals their enthusiasm for a crusade to overthrow the Papacy, the absolute monarchies of Europe and the Turkish Empire, whilst their programme of social, legal and economic reforms resembled in many respects those of the Levellers and the early Quakers. What was distinctive in their beliefs has been defined as follows: (1) 'Millenarianism formed the basic core of their doctrine, and was indeed the *raison d'être* of the movement.' (2) They claimed 'the right and indeed the duty of taking arms to overthrow existing regimes and establish the millennium'. (3) They put forward a 'detailed formulation of the political, social and economic structure of the promised kingdom'. (4) They expected 'this kingdom to arise from amongst the saints, ordinary citizens and soldiers'.⁵

The demand for the establishment of the Rule of the Saints was first put forward in February 1649, when the execution of Charles I seemed to have left the throne vacant for King Jesus. The demand was put forward by a number of Norfolk churches, which proposed that parliament should be elected by the congregational churches.⁶ As it became evident that the Rump would not adopt this programme an organised Fifth Monarchist movement emerged, which transferred its hopes to Cromwell and the army. It welcomed the dissolution of the Rump and the establishment of the Little Parliament, selected from a list of persons nominated by the congregational churches, but when radical proposals for legal reforms and the abolition of tithes were put forward the parliament was hastily dissolved. Instead Cromwell was installed as Lord Protector, and henceforward the Fifth Monarchists saw in him the betrayer of the revolution. After the establishment of the Protectorate they remained permanently in opposition, except for a brief interlude in 1659 when some of them supported the restored Rump. An extremist faction led by Thomas Venner in 1657 plotted a rebellion, which was prevented only at the last minute, and in 1661 Venner and about fifty of his followers rose in arms and for a few days terrorised London. These were the only attempts at a purely Fifth Monarchist revolt, but individual supporters of the movement co-operated with other Dissenters and republicans in almost every conspiracy and rebellion under Charles II and James II: Tong's plot in 1662, the Yorkshire plot in 1663, Rathbone's plot of 1665, the insurrection or 'Rye House' plot of 1682–3 and Monmouth's rebellion, as well as a conspiracy in Virginia in 1663.⁷

The Fifth Monarchists were a movement rather than a sect, differing among themselves on theological questions. Some were Calvinists, some Arminians; some favoured infant baptism, some believers' baptism; some observed the Sabbath on Sunday, others on Saturday; some believed that Christ's Second Coming would usher in the Millennium, others that he would not return until the Saints had established God's kingdom on Earth. Although there were a few Fifth Monarchist congregations, most of the movement's adherents were members of Independent or Baptist churches. A manifesto issued by London Fifth Monarchists in 1654 was signed by the whole congregations of two churches and individual members of eight others. When the Baptist church led by John Simpson split in 1657 over his repudiation of violence, seventy-two of its members broke away and formed a separate Fifth Monarchist church. After Venner's revolt, when Fifth Monarchists were hunted down as potential rebels, they seem to have gone underground, forming fractions inside existing churches. The persecution from which all Dissenters suffered won them followers; the movement which had sprung from the hopes of the 1640s and 1650s drew new strength from despair. Their theological differences were an asset, as they allowed individual supporters to penetrate Independent, Particular Baptist or General Baptist churches, and members of all three sects to accept Fifth Monarchist views. As John Rogers told Cromwell in 1655, 'that Fifth-Monarchy principle, as you call it, is of such a latitude as takes in all Saints, all such as are sanctified in Christ Jesus, without respect of what form or judgment he is'.[8]

When Terrill was converted to Fifth Monarchism is uncertain, though it was not later than 1670. He was already interested in eschatology in 1654, when he was terrified by a prophecy that the world would end two years later, and may have been influenced by a Fifth Monarchist agent, George Packer, who was active in Bristol in 1657.[9] The references to Cromwell in the *Records*, which are consistent with Fifth Monarchist beliefs, were written in the 1670s and do not necessarily represent his views twenty years earlier. The circumstances of his election as an elder in 1667 suggest that by then he was a Fifth Monarchist. They do not however constitute proof.

Following the death of the senior ruling elder of Broadmead, Terrill and Richard White were nominated to succeed him. The pastor, Thomas Ewins, and the surviving elder, Thomas Ellis, supported White, 'an humble, self-denying man' and probably easy to manipulate. However, the rest of the congregation voted solidly in favour of Terrill. A clash between the members and the leadership was averted only through the tact of a visiting minister, who suggested that both candidates should be declared elected. 'Seeing ye Election did not go according to their mindes', Terrill sardonically noted in the *Records*, Ewins and Ellis 'tooke hold' of this proposal, which was unanimously accepted.[10] If Terrill was known to be a Fifth Monarchist their hostility to his election is not difficult to explain, for a ruling elder holding extremist views might involve the church in serious trouble with the authorities.

When Ewins died in April 1670 Terrill wrote to 'that Eminent and worthy Servant of ye Lord', Vavasor Powell, asking for his help in finding a new pastor. Powell, an itinerant Welsh evangelist, had fought in the civil war and written a poem justifying Charles I's execution. After the establishment of the Protectorate he violently attacked Cromwell in his sermons, prophesied the imminence of the Fifth Monarchy, and told his congregation to go home and pray, 'Lord, wilt thou have Oliver Cromwell or Jesus Christ to reign over us?' Although he adopted a quietist position after the Restoration, he was repeatedly imprisoned for refusing to take the oaths of allegiance and supremacy. At the time of his correspondence with Terrill he was a prisoner in the Fleet, where he died in the following October. That Terrill applied to such a firebrand for advice on the choice of a pastor suggests that he hoped to bring about a Fifth Monarchist take-over at Broadmead.[11]

In his letter he mentioned Thomas Hardcastle, Powell's brother-in-law, as a possible minister. Powell approved, but pointed out that the London congregation of which Hardcastle was a member might not be willing to release him. Soon after Hardcastle was imprisoned for six months, which caused further delay. In the interim Robert Browne, whom Richard Baxter called 'a fervent, injudicious, honest Fifth-Monarchy-man' was invited to become pastor of Broadmead if Hardcastle was not available. Terrill's letters to him have been lost, but in his reply to one of them Browne wrote: 'The opening of the seal I must, for good reasons, as you will say, reserve till I see you.'[12] Apparently Terrill had detected signs of the fulfilment of the prophecy in *Revelation vi* of the opening of the seven seals, the coming of the four terrible horsemen and the great day of wrath; and Browne regarded the subject as too dangerous politically to be discussed in a letter.

After some hesitation Hardcastle accepted Broadmead's invitation. Terrill's eagerness to secure his services and Powell's approval suggest that if not a Fifth Monarchist he was at least sympathetic. The best clue to his thinking is supplied by twenty-two letters which he wrote to the church in 1675–6 while serving a prison sentence. The eighth of these is unmistakably millenarian in tone:

> But of all plagues, none like the locusts that come out of the bottomless pit, and the persecution that is kindled by the fire of hell. The plague of the beast and the whore, the beast and the false prophet, is the worst of all plagues; but for comfort see *Revelation xviii*. 4–8, and *xx*. 10. There are glorious prophecies to be fulfilled, and glorious promises to be accomplished. How comfortably may faith and patience live upon *Rev. xviii*. Read the whole chapter at your leisure.

It would be interesting to know how Hardcastle interpreted some of the prophecies to which he cryptically referred. *Revelation xiii* tells of a beast with seven heads, one of which receives a seemingly mortal wound but is afterwards healed, and of a second beast, later referred to as the false prophet, which makes men worship it. Hardcastle may have seen the monarchy in the first beast, the execution of Charles I in its wound, the Restoration in its healing, and the Church of England, which preached the divine right of kings, in the second beast or false prophet. He was apparently comforting his persecuted flock, which would understand his coded message, with the 'glorious promise' that the monarchy (the beast), the Church of Rome (the whore) and the church of England (the false prophet) would shortly be destroyed. In his fourteenth letter he foretold that the Second Coming was imminent: 'Yet a little while, and he that shall come will come, and will not tarry.' Three weeks later he enlarged on this theme:

Lord Jesus comes apace, salvation draws near: it is but a very little while and we shall be in the possession of it...Methinks, says faith, I see the wicked tumbling down, and calling on the mountains to cover them; and saying to the rocks, *Fall on us, and hide us*, &c, *Revelation vi.* 15; and the saints singing the new song, *Revelation v.* 9, 10.

The texts to which he refers foretell that the kings and great men of the earth will flee from the wrath of the Lamb, and that the Saints will reign on earth.[13] In the light of this evidence it is clear that Hardcastle was a millenarian and probably a Fifth Monarchy Man.

Another passage in his correspondence may be relevant here. Colonel Thomas Blood and Robert Perrot were arrested in 1671 after attempting to steal the crown, but were later released and pardoned. In a letter to Terrill written from London Hardcastle reported: 'Blood and Perrot are at full liberty, and, some say, without prejudice to any honest man done or to be done.'[14] Perrot was a Fifth Monarchy Man, and Hardcastle had apparently feared that his release had been conditional on his supplying information on his co-religionists or acting as a spy on them.

Precursors and portents

Four passages in the *Records* are of particular interest as indications of Terrill's thinking in the 1670s: his references to John Canne, the Münster Anabaptists, Cromwell, and the comets of 1664–5. He states that a leading part in the foundation of the Broadmead church was played by the Fifth Monarchist John Canne during a visit to Bristol in 1640. He describes Canne as 'a *Baptized* man' and 'a man very eminent in his day for Godlinesse, and for Reformation in Religion, haveing great understanding in ye way of ye Lord'.[15] In fact, Canne was not a Baptist, and in 1640 was not in England. If he did visit Bristol it was probably in 1648, when the future Broadmead church was already well established. Terrill's admiration for Canne's Fifth Monarchist activities led him to exaggerate his contribution to Broadmead.

Canne, who served as pastor of an English separatist congregation at Amsterdam from 1630 to 1647, defended the execution of Charles I in a pamphlet as 'Gods work, don in Gods way'. Appointed chaplain to the governor of Hull in 1650, he headed a Fifth Monarchist church there, and in 1653 published a pamphlet prophesying that God would 'eminently appear...overthrowing the Thrones of Kingdoms every where'. He was expelled in 1656 from Hull, where his propaganda was infecting the garrison and the fleet, and came to London. In *The Time of the End*, published in

1657 with introductions by the Fifth Monarchist preachers Christopher Feake and John Rogers, he denounced the Protectorate as the beast in *Revelation*, and declared that the time was nigh when the saints would proclaim war upon Babylon. After the Restoration he returned to Amsterdam, where he died. Terrill's admiration for Canne tells us a great deal about him.[16]

He probably assumed that Canne had received adult baptism because he was denounced in his lifetime as an Anabaptist. The Münster Anabaptists in 1534–5, under the leadership of Jan Bockelson (John of Leyden), had practised communism and polygamy; hence 'Anabaptist' was applied as a term of abuse to all religious and political radicals, whether Baptists, Fifth Monarchists, Levellers or Quakers, who were accused of planning to introduce similar practices. Fifth Monarchists disagreed in their views on the Münster Anabaptists. Some condemned them, including Canne, an unscrupulous propagandist, who compared the Levellers to John of Leyden's followers. Some pointed out that as all the evidence against them came from their enemies it was not reliable, whilst others regarded them with approval. The resolutions adopted by a series of Fifth Monarchist meetings in 1656 praised the work of John of Leyden, and called on the saints to 'visibly appear in a military posture for Christ'. Terrill in the *Records* adopted the intermediate position, explaining that:

> persons in ye practice of that truth of baptism were by some rendered very obnoxious; because, about 100 years before, some beyond ye sea, in Germany, that held that truth of Believers' baptisme, did (as some say) doe some very irregular actions; of whom we can have no true Accompt what they were but by *their Enimys*; for none but such in any History have made any relation or Narrative of them.

In view of 'those grosse Calumnies and untruths' spread about Dissenters in his own day, he thought himself justified in keeping an open mind on the question.[17]

In the *Records* he adopts the same critical attitude towards Cromwell as Powell and Canne, referring to him as 'Oliver Cromwell, called Lord Protector when as God alone was the Protector of his people; (*but we sinned*)'. The last phrase might imply either that Cromwell was sent as a punishment for the people's sins or that those who accepted the Protectorate sinned. Terrill's condemnation of him is mild compared with that of the Fifth Monarchists of the 1650s, however. Having experienced twelve years of intermittent persecution since the Restoration, he looked back with regret to 'those *Oliverian* dayes of Liberty'.[18]

Between December 1664 and March 1665 three comets were seen over Bristol on which Ewins made notes, whether from scientific curiosity or because he regarded them as portents. After his death these fell into Terrill's hands and suggested his comments in the *Records*, written about 1676, which provide a fascinating glimpse into the working of his mind:

> Ye first Starr's taile lay West north-West, by my apprehension, which might point out England (which lyeth so off ye Continent); and God's Judgments were sore upon it. Presently, by ye Greate Plague that followed in ye Ano. 1665, and by destroying ye Metropolitan Citty by fire, Ano. 1666, and by Warr with ye Dutch, wherein we, this nation, sustained greate losse. I gather, (by said Mr Ewin's figure of ye said Starrs), that ye second Starr's Taile lay East and by North East, which might point out Holland and Germany. And did not there follow sore desolations upon Holland, and ye lower part of ye Emperor's Country? Ye Third Starr's Taile, I perceive (by as aforesaid), lay South South-East; and doth not that Point out Fraunce and Spaine? but Fraunce Especially, that it may be ye Lord showed us l should taste of ye Third Cup, (after England and Holland); and by ye manner of ye Third Starr's appearing and abideing, who knows but it shows that their, viz. Fraunce's trouble shall continue untill ye daylight of ye Protestant Interest appear, and breake forth, to ye daylight of God's fulfilling his glorious promises in ye Holy Scriptures, to a visible manifestation of God's hastening ye Pulling downe of ye Papal Power and ye Pope? Amen; soe come, Lord Jesus.

Few of Terrill's contemporaries would have queried his assumption that the first comet foretold the Great Plague, the Great Fire of London and the Second Dutch war, and the second the French invasion of Holland in 1672 and the devastation of the Palatinate two years later. His millenarian views are more apparent in his interpretation of the third as a portent of the imminent chastisement of France and Spain, the bulwarks of the papacy, which was to be followed in the near future by the overthrow of the papal Babylon and the Second Coming of Christ.[19]

Anatomy of a Fifth Monarchist

It is worth considering why Terrill, a prosperous businessman, adopted Fifth Monarchist views. Although the movement attracted a few of the gentry and clergy and some professional men, the majority its supporters were journeymen and apprentices, especially in the textile industries. John Rogers' followers in London were described by a hostile witness as 'a handful of Scum, the very Haff of 20 Billingsgate, Redriffe, Ratcliff, Wappen, &c'.[20] Several reasons for Terrill's millenarianism, theological, political and personal, can be suggested. He was a strong Calvinist, and from the doctrine of predestination it was a logical inference that God willed the elect to rule over the reprobate. It was extremely doubtful whether all those holding office under the Commonwealth and Protectorate had been of the elect, and after the Restoration there could be no doubt whatever that the reprobate were firmly in the saddle. If Terrill adopted Fifth Monarchist views in the 1660s rather than the 1650s, this consideration must have weighed heavily with him.

It is no aspersion on the sincerity of his beliefs to suggest that he may have been influenced by personal frustration. Bristol was governed by a tightly knit oligarchy, most of them drawn from the wealthiest merchants. The twelve aldermen and thirty councillors held office for life, vacancies being filled by co-option and the same group largely controlled the city's economic life through the Society of Merchant Venturers. As the Corporation Act excluded Dissenters from local authorities, Terrill, whose ability as an organiser and administrator was demonstrated by his business career and his church activities, was denied any opportunity to exercise his talents in public life. Instead he found himself ruled by men such as Sir Robert Yeamans and Ralph Ollive, whom he despised as drunkards.[21]

To suggest that he was motivated solely by personal ambition would be unjust. Although the Fifth Monarchists were not democrats, the form of government which they advocated would probably have been more democratic than the existing system. The Rule of the Saints would have replaced the rule of the gentry and rich merchants by that of 'the middle sort of people'. Forming the bulk of the members of the Dissenting churches, these included small businessmen and professional men such as Terrill, shopkeepers, artisans and peasant farmers. The members of Broadmead in Terrill's day were such people. They included men like Ellis, Robert Bodenham and Terrill himself who were in comfortable circumstances, but also others such as the journeyman shoemaker Henry Pierce, 'a very meane poore man to appearance in Person and habit…that lived up in a Cockloft'.[22] It was such men as the male members of Broadmead, a cross-section of the middle and lower middle classes, who if Terrill had had his way would have been elected and sat in the House of Commons and Bristol's Common Council.

In September 1678 Titus Oates denounced his Popish Plot to the Privy Council. At Broadmead's monthly prayer meeting on 5 November, the anniversary of a more genuine plot, the congregation sang a hymn which

Terrill had written for the occasion, beginning

> As papists still do seek to kill
> the governors of our land;
> The Lord of might, doth bring to light,
> the plots they take in hand.

Nine more verses followed, more than enough to make it clear that he was no poet. The episode is significant as evidence that hymns were sometimes sung at Broadmead, even if only on special occasions. Congregational hymn-singing was a Fifth Monarchist practice, whereas both Anglican and most Dissenting congregations normally sang only metrical versions of the psalms. Among the Fifth Monarchist leaders Powell, Feake and Rogers all wrote hymns, although only Rogers showed any ability to rise above doggerel. A report on his conduct while imprisoned in 1654–5 states: 'Take notice of his self-made hymns, read by him, and publicly sung by him and his society for divine service.' It continued: 'This one verse for pattern':

> For God begins to honour us.
>   The saints are marching on;
> The sword is sharp, the arrows swift
>   To destroy Babylon.
> Against the kingdom of the Beast
>   We witnesses do rise, &c.

The association of hymn-singing with millenarians such as the Fifth Monarchists, antinomians such as the Muggletonians and 'enthusiasts' such as the Moravians and Methodists largely explains why the practice did not become common among Dissenters before 1750, or in the Church of England until early Victorian days.[23]

Death and persecutions

Thomas Hardcastle died suddenly and unexpectedly on 29 September 1678, and on 17 December, Terrill noted in the *Records*, 'ye Church took it into Consideration about getting a pasteur. Several were discoursed of, as Mr Ralphson, Mr Founds of London. But they concluded to send a letter to Mr Robert Browne.' An invitation to Browne was drafted on the same day and signed by Terrill, the deacons William Dickason and John Ford, and seven other members. As a reply was received from Browne's church that he could not be spared, it was agreed on 22 April 1679 to write to George Fownes. He accepted, and after setting his affairs in order in London took up his post on 9 November.[24]

Of the three men whose names were put forward, Browne had already been approached after Ewins' death. Ralphson, whose real name was Jeremiah Marsden, played an active part in the Yorkshire plot, and was described by an informer as 'a chief contriver of the conspiracy and a trusted agent of the separate Congregations and Anabaptists'. He spent the rest of his life on the run, and to avoid detection adopted the alias of Ralphson, Ralph being his father's Christian name. In 1669 he was reported to be 'preaching up the Fifth Anarchy', and to have said in a prayer, 'As for our rulers, what shall wee say unto thee O Lord? Our rulers are rulers of Sodome and of Gomorrah.' When he died in Newgate in 1684 his funeral, which was attended by 5,000 mourners, turned into a political demonstration. Fownes, a less controversial figure, acted as co-pastor with Anthony Palmer of a joint congregation of Independents and Baptists at Pinners' Hall, London. Palmer was a Fifth Monarchist, and in 1663 was said to be meeting Thomas Palmer (apparently no relation), another Fifth Monarchist who in collaboration with Marsden had played an active part in the Yorkshire plot. There is no direct evidence that Fownes was himself a Fifth Monarchist, but he co-operated closely with men who were.[25]

According to the *Records*, the Bristol Dissenters suffered six outbursts of persecution between December 1660 and July 1667, during which Ewins was imprisoned four times for periods varying from three weeks to almost a year. How much freedom of worship they enjoyed was determined by fluctuations in government policy and also by the attitude of the mayor and sheriffs. Sir John Knight the elder is described in the *Records* as 'a Tyrant', and his younger namesake and Sir Thomas Earle as 'great Persecutors'. On the other hand, John Willoughby, Alderman John Knight and Sir Robert Canne are praised as 'Moderate men' who 'did winke at our thus meeting'. A more effective persecution began in May 1670 after the passing of the Second Conventicle Act. The trained bands were employed to nail up the doors of the meeting houses every Saturday evening, so that the Broadmead members 'were faine to meet in ye Lanes and highways for severall months'. In these circumstances it is not surprising that some Dissenters began to think in terms of revolt. The mayor, Sir Robert Yeamans, wrote to Lord Arlington on 21 May: 'The factious party are more numerous than the loyal, and although of different persuasions, they unite in conversation, and seem so discontented that little less than rebellion is to be read in their faces and gestures.'[26] Although Yeamans exaggerated the danger, the authorities had real cause for concern, for there were many former New Model Army officers and soldiers in Bristol's Dissenting churches, including Broadmead.

The eighth persecution began in October 1674 at the instigation of the bishop, Guy Carleton. After the licences to preach granted to Dissenting ministers in 1672 had been revoked, Hardcastle, the Independent minister John Thompson and the Presbyterian minister John Weekes were arrested in February 1675. Appeals for the release of Thompson, who was in poor health, were rejected by Carleton, and three weeks later he died in prison. His death aroused great indignation among the Dissenters, some 5,000 of whom attended his funeral on 5 March. The local postmaster informed the government on the following day that:

> shortly after Thompson's burial, a libel was found in the Mayor's house with these threatening expressions or to this purpose, that, if they must be subject to these persecutions, as they term it, there were many eminent and sufficient men, and numbers of apprentices and inferior rank would venture their lives and fortunes for their freedom, and 'tis probable that of this city two parts of three may be that way inclined.

Hardcastle and Weekes were released in August, but Hardcastle was again arrested a few days later and sentenced to a further six months' imprisonment, during which he wrote the letters to his church quoted above.[27]

The longest period of persecution began in July 1680, and apart from a brief pause between August and November 1681 continued until the early months of 1686. Although persecution was general during this period, it was particularly intense in Bristol, which contained a higher proportion of Dissenters in its population than any other city, and had a reputation for being 'even as factious as it is great and populous'. The Dissenters' meeting houses were wrecked, and they were, forced to worship in the fields and woods. Many were imprisoned, heavily fined or had their goods distrained. When in April 1683 a Presbyterian open-air service was broken up by constables, one man was driven into the river and drowned. The grand jury charged those responsible with murder, but on the judge's orders the charges were quashed.[28]

Persecution inevitably provoked the treasonable activities it was supposedly intended to prevent. Nathaniel Wade, a Bristol barrister, was accused in 1680 of being the leader of about sixty Dissenters who had 'formed themselves into an armed company and had several meetings, where they exercised themselves in arms'. Whatever the truth of this report, he certainly played a leading part in the plan formed in 1682 for simultaneous uprisings in London, Bristol and other centres. He swore in October 1685, when he was a prisoner after Monmouth's rebellion, that only five Bristolians besides himself had known of the preparations for a rising in the city. These were his brother William Wade, Joseph Tiley, James Holloway, Thomas Tyler and Benjamin Adlam. Of these Holloway, Adlam and Tyler had already been executed, and William Wade and Tiley were safely out of the country. Almost certainly others had been involved whom he was trying to shield. Holloway after his arrest in 1684 had named Samuel Jacob as another member of the 'cabal of conspiracy in Bristol', but Wade did not mention him, presumably because he was still at large.[29]

All those named except Tiley certainly or possibly had associations with Dissenting churches. The Wades were members of the Castle Hill Independent church, of which John Hellier, a Bristol attorney, wrote in 1683 that:

> all the disorders here and all the seditious (perhaps treasonable) contrivances against his Majesty and the government were hatched in that meeting-house and thence derived into coffee-houses and clubs.

They also had links with Broadmead, of which their mother had been a member; Nathaniel is referred to in the *Records* as 'a friend'. Jacob was a Presbyterian, and Adlam probably a member of the Pithay Particular Baptist church. Tyler may have been the son of Thomas and Sarah Tyler, two elderly members of Broadmead, and there is some evidence that he had Fifth Monarchist leanings. Although Holloway claimed on the scaffold to be a Churchman, Hellier alleged that he was a member of the Castle Hill church. The conspirators, according to Holloway, the accuracy of whose confession was confirmed by Wade, concluded that 'the only way to secure Bristol would be by a surprize, which with about 350 (150 of whom we depended on from Taunton, the other 200 to be raised in and about the city) might easily be done'. Bristol's two Whig clubs, the Horseshoe Club, which had about 120 members, and the Mermaid Club, would have supplied some of the required two hundred, but the bulk of them would have had to come from the Dissenting congregations from which in any case the clubs largely drew their membership.[30]

If Broadmead was a Fifth Monarchist centre, why were none of its members among the conspirators? One explanation may be that millenarianism could take either an active or a passive form. The Fifth Monarchist might believe it his duty to take up arms to hasten the coming of Christ's kingdom, or he might prefer to await the divine intervention which he believed to be imminent. Vavasor Powell seems to have moved from a militant to a quietist position; in 1661 he wrote that he saw no scriptural warrant 'to affirm, that there are no Magistrates now in being in the World, or that the Magistrates, under and belonging to the fourth Monarchy, are not to be obey'd'. His admirer Terrill and other members of Broadmead may have adopted a similar position. That does not necessarily mean that none of them took part in the plot. Wade's list of conspirators was certainly incomplete, and some facts suggest that Broadmead may have been involved. The coffee-house next to the Tolzey, which was said in 1681 to be 'frequented by many schismatical, seditious and disloyal persons', was run by a church member, Anne Kimbar.[31]

In June 1684 a new charter was issued which in effect gave the king complete control of the government of Bristol. As it was feared that public resentment might lead to riots, the houses of 'dangerous and disaffected persons' were searched for arms. Weapons were seized from Terrill, who lost a musket, a pike and a sword; from Daniel Gwilliam, who was to succeed him as ruling elder; from Robert Bodenham and William Dickason, the deacons of the church; from several other members of Broadmead; from John Mott, a working partner in the sugar refinery; Anthony Wood, its manager; and Michael Pope, who had taken over the business in 1682; from members of the Castle Hill, Pithay and Presbyterian churches and one Quaker; and from two of the 1682–3 conspirators, Adlam and Jacob. These discoveries did not necessarily have a political significance, for in the absence of an effective police force everyone with any property to lose kept some sort of weapon in the house. From almost all the houses searched not more than three weapons were seized, but two large caches of arms were discovered. Bodenham was found to possess twenty-seven firearms and nine swords. Broadmead had a little over forty male members in 1684, and the houses searched contained enough weapons to arm them all. If the Dissenting churches were to have taken part in the planned rising, Bodenham may have been responsible for the custody of the arms for the Broadmead contingent. The other cache, consisting of two firearms, two swords and twenty-seven 'muskets which were taken at gunsmiths', was in the possession of Thomas Scroop or Scrope, the son of the regicide Colonel Adrian Scroop, who was a leading member of the Castle Hill church and presumably custodian of its stock of weapons.[32]

Fifth Monarchy Men may have played a larger part in Monmouth's rebellion than is generally assumed. There were at least three among Monmouth's officers: Lieutenant-Colonel Samuel Venner, Thomas Venner's son; Captain John Patchall, who had been involved in the 1661 revolt, the Yorkshire plot and the 1682 insurrection plot; and Major Robert Perrot, the crown-stealer, who had also been involved in the 1682 plot. With Fifth Monarchists so well represented among the officers, it is unlikely that there were none among the rank and file. Patchall was killed in battle and Perrot executed, but Venner escaped to the Netherlands, where he continued to plot. An informer reported that a faction among the exiles including Venner, who was threatening to avenge his father's death, expected the overthrow of Babylon and the inauguration of Christ's kingdom within three years, and that 'these doe of their absolute power down into the pitt of hell all those that possesse five hundred pounds a year; they are of the rich that cant be saved'.[33]

The Western Martyrology or Bloody Assizes, published in five editions between 1689 and 1705, contains two hymns which may have a bearing on the question of Fifth Monarchist participation in Monmouth's rebellion. One is said to have been written before his execution by Thomas Tyler, the Bristol conspirator, who had served in Monmouth's army as a lieutenant. Two of its seven verses can be interpreted in Fifth Monarchist terms:

> Appear for those that plead thy Cause,
> Preserve them in the Way,
> Who own King Jesus and his Laws
> And dare not but obey.
> O God confound our cruel Foes,
> Let Babylon come down;
> Let England's king be one of them
> Shall rase her to the Ground.

Here the references to King Jesus and the destruction of Babylon are Fifth Monarchist commonplaces. 'King Jesus and the heads upon the gates!' was the battlecry of the 1661 rising. The prayer that a king of England should take part in a crusade against the papacy was probably suggested by the prophecy in *Revelation xvii* that Babylon would be overthrown by ten kings, before they in turn were conquered by the Lamb. *The Western Martyrology* also gives three hymns said to have been written by 'several Worthy Persons that were Prisoners for the Sake of Christ', apparently victims of the Bloody Assizes. One of these, a prophecy of the imminent downfall of Babylon, seems to be the work of a Fifth Monarchy Man among Monmouth's followers. Three of the nine verses run:

> Set up thy Standard and prepare
> War against Babylon:

For her Destruction draweth near,
As here we read her Doom…

But Babel must drink up the Dregs
Of Wrath which do remain,
With which no Mixture she shall have
To mitigate her Pain.

For 'tis the Vengeance of our God,
And of his Temple too,
The Vials that fill up his Wrath,
The Three Last Trumpets Woe.

'Set up thy Standard' echoes the title of the manifesto issued by Thomas Venner in 1657, *A Standard Set Up*. The intense hatred of popery expressed in the hymn suggests that it might have been written in prison by a Fifth Monarchist awaiting execution or transportation.[34]

Unfulfilled prophecies

The Bristol Dissenters on whom the 1682–3 conspirators had relied were denied the opportunity to take part in Monmouth's rebellion by his decision to turn back from the city. Contemporary accounts suggest that if he had attacked many of them would have rallied to his support. An anonymous source obviously writing from inside knowledge reported:

> some gentlemen that came over with us, and were proscrib'd on account of the former plot [i.e. Wade and Tiley], being Bristol men, and knew the hearts of the townsmen, begg'd him heartily to proceed towards it, offering themselves to go in at the head of them into the town, by some private ways which they knew, assuring him they would make no resistance.

Wade confirmed in his confession that Tiley had assured Monmouth that 'most of the Cityzens were for him'. From inside the city Monmouth received a similar assurance from Andrew Gifford, the pastor of Pithay and a friend of Terrill, who according to his grandson:

> was with several others in the City of Bristol, deeply engaged in the affair of the Duke of Monmouth. He collected a considerable sum, and provided ammunition. And when the Duke came near the city he sent his

son to Knowl Castle, a mile out of the city, to invite the Duke and his friends in; assuring him that there were many friends and supplies provided, and that a part of the city walls was undermined to let them in with ease and safety.

If Monmouth had had sufficient determination to attack Bristol, the Dissenters' co-operation might well have given him control of the city, and thereby assured the success of the rebellion.[35]

Between 1685 and 1689 the Fifth Monarchist movement suffered a series of major setbacks, both at Broadmead and nationally. After nearly three years' imprisonment Fownes died in Gloucester jail on 29 November 1685, whilst Terrill died in the later months of 1684 or in 1685. There is no evidence that either David Gwilliam, who was elected ruling elder in July 1686 'in ye place of dear Br. Terrill, decd.', or Thomas Vaux, who was elected pastor in April 1687, was a Fifth Monarchist.[36]

Monmouth's rebellion probably took a heavy toll among the Fifth Monarchists. In addition to those killed in battle, executed or forced to go into exile, there were almost certainly some among the hundreds who died in prison or were transported. When Bevil Skelton, the English envoy at The Hague, was informed in October 1686 of a conspiracy among the Fifth Monarchist exiles, he contemptuously dismissed them as 'Insignificant—in number inconsiderable'. The cessation of persecution after 1686, by removing the Dissenters' worst grievance, deprived the Fifth Monarchists of their mass basis. By 1689 all the older leaders of the movement—Simpson, Rogers, Canne, Powell, Anthony Palmer, Feaker Marsden and Browne—had died, and younger men were not coming forward to replace them.

The basic problem was that there had been too many unfulfilled prophecies. None of the marvels so confidently foretold for the 1650s and 1660s had materialised, and predictions that the millennium would begin in 1688, 1694, 1695, 1700 or 1701 all proved equally unfounded. A millenarian tradition lingered on in London throughout the eighteenth century, from the sect of Millenaries recorded in 1706 to the Millennium Press in Spitalfields, which eighty years later was still issuing pamphlets predicting the imminence of the Fifth Monarchy. The early Methodists, Blake and Coleridge were all influenced by millenarian ideas. It was not until the new situation produced by the French and industrial revolutions had given rise to the mass movements associated with Richard Brothers and Joanna Southcott, however, that millenarianism again became a cause for serious concern to the authorities.

The common belief that the Fifth Monarchist movement 'rapidly disintegrated after 1660' is probably mistaken. The evidence suggests that up to

1685 it remained a political force to be reckoned with. Its influence has been underestimated because it preferred to operate in semi-secrecy inside Independent and Baptist churches. Under the guidance of Terrill, the admirer of Canne and correspondent of Powell and Browne, Broadmead seems to have come under Fifth Monarchist control from 1670 to 1685, and a similar story could probably be told of other congregations.

Notes

1. The standard edition is that by Roger Hayden, published by the Bristol Record Society (Bristol, 1974). The earlier edition by Edward Bean Underhill, published by the Hanserd Knollys Society (London, 1847), contains additional documents, including Terrill's account of his conversion, his hymn on the Popish Plot, Ewins' diagram of the comets of 1664–5, Browne's letters to Terrill and Hardcastle's letters to his church.
2. Cal. State Papers Dom., Jas. II, I, p.335.
3. Hayden, *Records*, pp.5–9.
4. Hayden, *Records*, pp.128–9, 194–8, 213–18.
5. S. Capp, *The Fifth Monarchy Men* (London, 1972), pp.14, 22.
6. A. S. P. Woodhouse (ed.), *Puritanism and Liberty* (London, 1938), pp.245–6.
7. Capp, *Fifth Monarchy Men*, pp.209–11, 220–1; Richard L. Greaves, *Deliver Us from Evil: The Radical Undersround in Britain, 1660–1663* (Oxford, 1986), pp.115–16, 119, 122, 166–7, 177–9, 181, 184; Greaves, *Secrets of the Kingdom: British radicals from the Popish Plot to the Revolution of 1688–89* (Stanford, Cal., 1992), p.183; Peter Linebaugh and Marcus Rediker, *The Many-Headed Hydra* (London, 2000), p.135.
8. Capp, *Fifth Monarchy Men*, pp.105, 272, 276–8; Edward Rogers, *Some Account of the Life and Opinions of a Fifth-Monarchy-Man* (London, 1867), p.215.
9. Underhill, *Records*, p.60; Thurloe State Papers (London, 1742), pp.vi, 187.
10. Hayden, *Records*, pp.122–3, 309.
11. Hayden, *Records*, p.129; Capp, Fifth Monarchy Men, pp.101, 112–3, 134–5; P. G. Rogers, *The Fifth Monarchy Men* (Oxford, 1966), pp. 40–2, 68, 130.
12. A.G. Matthews, *Calamy Revised* (Oxford, 1934), p.81; Underhill, *Records*, p.131.
13. Matthews, *Calamy Revised*, pp.285, 316, 328.
14. Matthews, *Calamy Revised*, p.156.
15. Hayden, *Records*, p.90.
16. Capp, *Fifth Monarchy Men*, pp.51, 53, 115; Rogers, *Fifth Monarchy Men*, p.91.
17. Capp, *Fifth Monarchy Men*, pp.116, 145–6; Hayden, *Records*, p.91.
18. Hayden, *Records*, pp.106–7.
19. Hayden, *Records*, p.120.
20. Rogers, *Life and Opinions*, p.169.
21. Hayden, *Records*, pp.145, 174.
22. Hayden, *Records*, p.136.
23. Underhill, *Records*, p.389; L. F. Brown, *Baptists and Fifth Monarchy Men* (Oxford, 1912), p.51; Rogers, *Life and Opinions*, p.171; Hiller Schwartz, *The French Prophets*

(Berkeley, Cal., 1980), p.260; Ian Bradley, *Abide with Me* (London, 1997), pp.1–2, 7–22.
24. Hayden, *Records*, pp.203, 205–6, 209–12, 219.
25. Matthews, *Calamy Revised*, pp.210, 339, 380; Capp, *Fifth Monarchy Men*, p.218.
26. Hayden, *Records*, pp.116–22, 125, 127–8, 170, 265; Cal. State Papers Dom., Chas. II, x, pp.229–30.
27. Hayden, *Records*, pp.144–5, 148–50, 166–7, 183; Cal. State Papers Dom., Chas. II, xvii, p.10.
28. Hayden, *Records*, pp.220–2, 227–66; Cal. State Papers Dom., Chas. II, xviii, p.51.
29. Cal. State Papers Dom., Chas. II, xxi, p.597; W. MacDonald Wigfield, *The Monmouth Rebellion* (Bradford-on-Avon, 1980), 153–4; Cal. State Papers Dom., Chas. II, xxvi, p.238.
30. Cal. State Papers Dom. Chas. II, xxv, pp.165–6, 250, 266; Hayden, *Records*, pp.201, 222, 238, 251; *Cobbett's Complete Collection of State Trials* (London, 1811), x, col. 26.
31. Capp, *Fifth Monarchy Men*, pp.134–5; Jonathan Barry, 'The Politics of Religion in Restoration Bristol', in Tim Harris, Paul Seaward and Mark Goldie (ed.), *The Politics of Religion in Restoration England* (Oxford, 1990), p.175; Hayden, *Records*, p.297; Cal. State Papers Dom., Chas. II, xxii, p.251.
32. *Transactions of the Bristol and Gloucestershire Archaeological Society*, ii (1877–8), pp.105–13; xlv (1944), p.38.
33. Greaves, *Secrets of the Kingdom*, pp.298–9.
34. J. G. Muddiman (ed.), *The Bloody Assizes* (Edinburgh, 1929), pp.88–9, 123–5. Tyler's Christian name is given incorrectly as Joseph, probably because the compiler confused him with his fellow-Bristolian Joseph Tiley.
35. Muddiman, Bloody Assizes, p.167; Wigfield, *Monmouth Rebellion*, p.152; Hayden, *Records*, p.71.
36. Hayden, *Records*, pp.265–6.
37. Greaves, *Secrets of the Kingdom*, p.313; E.P. Thompson, *Witness Against the Beast* (Cambridge, 1993), pp.53, 55; Donald Davie, *The Eighteenth-Century Hymn in England* (Cambridge, 1993), p.69.
38. Christopher Hill, *England's Turning Point* (London, 1998), p.134.

Forum
Alternative greatest Britons?

Should we give credence to such ideas as there being a 'greatest Briton'? Following the BBC television series giving viewers just ten contenders to choose from, and coming up with the verdict that there was a greatest Briton and that his name was Churchill, we asked some of our readers and supporters whose names they would have added to the list. Here are some of their answers. Further nominations are welcomed and will be posted on the *Socialist History* website!

The 'forum' section will be a regular feature of *Socialist History*, edited by Andy Croft. In our next issue it will feature an exchange between Andy and regular *SH* contributor John Newsinger on the political significance of George Orwell. Any suggestions for future themes and contributions should be sent to andy.croft@ntlworld.com.

William Blake

'My Mother groan'd, my Father wept/ Into the dangerous World I leapt'—that's how William Blake was born in London in 1757. For sixty-nine years he worked as a great poet, a visionary, a painter, an engraver, helped by his beloved wife Catherine. Because of his originality and his refusal to bow to commercial pressures, he lived in poverty—but his many friends described him as a happy man. He died a good death, composing songs as he lay in bed on a summer evening and singing them to Catherine. When she said she liked his songs, Blake said: 'They are not mine, my beloved, they are not mine.'

Blake often sang his poems to friends. He also printed them himself, creating picture poems which he printed off and coloured in for the few people who recognised his genius.

Politically he was not only ahead of his time, but far ahead of ours. I consider him the most advanced political writer of all. His vision of a New

Jerusalem, of mutual creative work, was not an abstract dream, but a practical proposition. The New Jerusalem is not an after-life promise, but a job to be undertaken right here and now:

> The fields from Islington to Marybone
> To Primrose Hill and Saint John's Wood
> Were builded over with pillars of gold
> And there Jerusalem's pillars stood
>
> In my exchanges every land
> Shall walk and mine in every land
> Mutual shall build Jerusalem
> Both heart in heart and hand in hand

Blake hated kings, warriors and priests. His poems attacked big business, slavery, sexism, war, child abuse, racism and poverty. No wonder that he was put on trial for sedition—for which he could have been hanged. (He managed to get off by telling a few white lies.)

Don't be put off by the obscurities in his *Prophetic Books*. Start by reading—aloud—his *Songs of Innocence and Experience* and his amazing *The Marriage of Heaven and Hell*. (Both are published in paperback with the original coloured designs: miniature stained glass windows depicting the brightness and darkness of the world.)

Blake went to school for only one day—he didn't like it, so he never went back. He educated himself and later attended drawing school. His religion and political beliefs were his own invention: 'I must invent a System, or be enslav'd by another man's', he wrote. He wrote many magical slogans—'The cut worm forgives the plow'; 'everything that lives is Holy'—that sound as simple as a glass of water. But you can explore them for the rest of your life.

Blake fits nobody's definitions. Of course he was a socialist—an anarchist; a pacifist and a revolutionary. Above all, he was a free spirit with a wicked sense of humour. His work and the example of his honest life prove that it is possible to live a good life in a corrupt society, that even under tyrannous governments it is possible to create areas of peace.

Adrian Mitchell is a poet, playwright and novelist. His celebration of William Blake's life and works, set to music composed by Mike Westbrook, was shown at the National Theatre, on TV and resulted in the jazz recording Glad Day: Settings of William Blake.

Percy Bysshe Shelley

Shelley's my man. If he were alive now he wouldn't be sitting in an ivory tower, only leaving to attend the odd literature festival, he would be demonstrating against the exploitation of the third world and performing at the Glastonbury festival. He would have marched with us on 15th February.

I used to think of Shelley as just another one of those dead white poets who wrote difficult poetry for difficult people, but then I learned how dedicated he was to justice and the liberation of the poor. He probably saw very few black people but he was passionately against the slave trade. It was this that turned me on to Shelley, his humanity, passion, and his rock-and-roll attitude. His ability to connect poetry to the concerns of everyday people was central to his poetic purpose, and those everyday people overstood that he did not simply do arts for art's sake: this was arts that was uncompromisingly revolutionary. He wrote for the masses. No TV, no radio, no Internet, but his poetry was being quoted on the streets and chanted at demonstrations; not only did Shelley know the power of poetry, more importantly, he knew the power of the people. I think of him as the 'Dub' poet of his time. The other thing is I think he was really fucking sexy; women loved him, the authorities hated him, and everyone knew when he was in town.

Shelley once said: 'My soul is bursting, ideas millions of ideas are crowding into it.' Hey, I feel like that sometimes but everybody tells me I should get therapy. Shelley also said: 'Let the axe strike the tree/the poison tree will fall.' He's right, I believe him. What can we do about our corrupt, deceitful politicians? How can we halt the evil arms trade? How can we make corporate tyrants pay for the crimes they do? I know, we should let the axe strike the tree and then the poison tree will fall. The guy's so relevant, the brother's so now.

Shelley was a 'great Briton' because he was an internationalist, he cared about the people of Italy, and Africa, as much as he cared about the people of Britain. He knew the role poetry and the arts could play in opening minds, and he has left us beautiful, angry, powerful, lyrical, revolutionary poetry. As well as being a visionary, in my humble opinion he can also be seen as the greatest poetic historian Britain has ever produced.

Benjamin Zephaniah is a poet and writer who grew up in Jamaica and Handsworth, Birmingham. In November 2003 he turned down an OBE, on the grounds that he is 'profoundly anti-empire'. He has written about Shelley and narrates The Shelley Story *on CD/cassette.*

Thomas Hepburn

In 1976 the Royal Mail issued a stamp in tribute to Thomas Hepburn (1796–1864), as part of a series commemorating important British social reformers. Yet despite this brief episode of national recognition the name of Thomas Hepburn is probably little known outside his native North-East. This is a pity. He deserves the title of a 'great Briton' both for his achievements and for the many ways in which he continues to be a source of inspiration and hope for people both in our region, and more widely, today.

My own constituency plays an important part in the perpetuation of Thomas Hepburn's memory. His grave is in Heworth Churchyard and the inscription reads: 'He initiated the first great union of Northern Miners in 1831 and conducted the strike of 1832 with great forbearance and ability. His life was spent in advocating shorter hours of Labour and extended education for miners'. Each year the National Union of Mineworkers in the North East holds a service in St Mary's Heworth to commemorate Hepburn's life and work, in which a national figure, normally from the trade union or labour movement, gives an address. A school in the constituency, appropriately in Felling since Hepburn worked for a while in Felling pit, is also named after him, as is a street on one of the estates in the area.

Hepburn' s qualities of leadership against injustice no doubt developed through years of experience of being a miner at Urpeth, Fatfield, Jarrow and Hetton. During this time he was exposed to the long hours, appalling conditions, low wages, and use of child labour prevalent in North East pits. He himself had begun work in the pit at the age of eight and, as the eldest of three children, had had to support his family in the absence of his father who had been killed in a mining accident. He emerged as a spokesman for miners at that crucial time when moves were first afoot to create a miners organisation, a Miners Union, in the North East coalfield. In 1831 it was Thomas Hepburn who led the first protest rallies, conducted the first strikes and founded the first pitmen's union.

They must have been stirring times. There were historic gatherings on the Black Fell near Birtley and on the Town Moor in Newcastle in 1831 when the men first formulated their demands and which led to the 1831 strike. These also constituted the establishment of organised trade unionism in the pits. It was through this activity that the miners also tasted their first victory; as a result of the dispute a twelve-hour day for boys was granted, the union was recognised, at least *de facto*, and it was agreed that outsiders were not to be brought in to work in the pits where local miners were unemployed.

Like many early trade union and labour movement reformers, Thomas Hepburn was a religious man, a Methodist who recommended to his fellow miners 'order, sobriety and attention to religious duties'. While he strongly attacked injustice he decried violent protest and did not hesitate to rebuke over-zealous or intolerant supporters. Perhaps because of this he won widespread public respect even among those who were unlikely to be natural sympathisers of the causes he espoused. Hepburn's Methodism was not austere, however, and his speeches show humour as well as conviction, calling, in his own words, for an outcome where 'there would be employment for every man, we would get bread to eat and sometimes get a little rum to drink!'

While justice for miners was his principal cause Hepburn also was active in the Chartist movement and the Northern Political Union, set up to support the Great Reform Bill and another eminent Northern reformer of the time, Earl Grey.

Hepburn's courage and leadership were never rewarded by any material success. Indeed, the economic penalties he suffered were considerable and because of his commitment to the cause of social and industrial reform he was doomed never to enjoy sustained financial or employment security. After the 1831 strike he was blacklisted and was reduced to a hand-to-mouth existence, surviving for a while as an itinerant tea-seller. Eventually, after a number of years of severe hardship, he was offered employment at Felling colliery but only on condition he was not engaged in union organisation. His working life ended through incapacity in 1859 and he died five years later, reportedly at the Brandy Butt, the pub on Newcastle's quayside run by his daughter and son-in-law.

The establishment of the union and the successful outcome of the 1831 strike were momentous events. While they were followed in the immediate years by setbacks—within a short period of time the employers had broken both a second strike and the infant union organisation—the seeds had been sown and were eventually to bear fruit.

Indeed I like to think that by the time Hepburn died in 1864 he would have been fully aware both of the new stirrings of trade unionism and the moves in parliament to adopt legislation on miners' safety and better working conditions in the mines and elsewhere. That he had unleashed a movement which was to gather a powerful momentum was, I believe, recognised by Hepburn himself as the following words from one of his later public speeches shows. 'the time will come when the golden chain which binds the tyrants together will be snapped, when men will be properly organized, when coal owners will only be like ordinary men, and will have to sigh for the days gone by. It only needs time to bring this about.'

Fortunately, Thomas Hepburn continues to be commemorated regularly in the region of his birth, so he could not be described as an unsung hero.

However, there is a long way to go, in my view, before his status as a truly great Briton is recognised to the extent it undoubtedly merits.

Joyce Quinn is Labour MP for Gateshead East and Washington West.

Eleanor Marx

Eleanor Marx was an intelligent and talented woman, a socialist, and an internationalist who lived by her beliefs. Born in London in 1855 as the sixth child of Jenny and Karl Marx, she grew up with strong family ties, later to flout convention by setting up home, unmarried, with the man she loved. She had a deep appreciation of literature, the theatre and poetry. Not surprisingly, she became immersed in politics from a young age, and the role of women in society exercised her greatly. Railing against married women becoming the 'property' of their husbands, she hated capitalist society where women could be so subjugated.

For a young, educated woman from an outwardly bourgeois family it was difficult to obtain work apart from small teaching jobs or researching in the British Museum for others-she did both, earning a pittance for working long hours. Her desire to become an actor caused a stir as being unsuitable for 'respectable ladies'. She firmly believed the economic emancipation of women was linked to the emancipation of the working class—a cause to which she enthusiastically dedicated her life.

A gifted linguist, her translations brought the writings of a host of internationally known socialist figures to the British labour movement through the pages of *Justice* and *Commonweal*. She also learnt Norwegian in order to translate Ibsen's *A Dolls House*, which became the standard translation for the next hundred years.

Having imbibed an impressive knowledge of economics, she gave lectures and classes for the Social Democratic Federation and later the Socialist League. Eleanor was one of the speakers at the first May Day demonstration in 1890. She gave active support to efforts to organise unskilled labour in the East End of London, playing a significant role in the Great Docks Strike and the formation of the Gasworkers' Union (now the GMB). A trade unionist herself, she became secretary of the Silvertown Women's Branch of the Gasworkers' Union. Union leader Will Thorne said that, had she lived, Eleanor 'would have been a greater women's leader than the greatest contemporary women'. Her encouragement and empowerment of unskilled workers into the 'New Union' movement of the 1890s was of lasting benefit. She died young and tragically, taking her own life after being betrayed by Edward Aveling—a great loss to the British and international labour movement.

Eleanor Marx was a rare and special being, according to her contemporaries, immortalised by Walter Crane as the spirit of May Day in his 1898 cartoon. She held her beliefs firmly and tried to live to them—a truly great Briton.

Tish Collins *is librarian of the Marx Memorial Library.*

Four contemporary 'great Britons'

I found it more difficult than I anticipated when I agreed to nominate a 'greatest Briton'. The reason is that my knowledge is limited. What do I really know about the achievements, difficulties overcome and the personal characteristics of human beings whose historical portraits I admire but who lived many years before my birth? Within this group I would certainly include John Ball, Wat Tyler, Winstanley, Tom Paine, Milton, Shelley, Robert Owen, Ernest Jones the Chartist leader, George Loveless of the Tolpuddle Martyrs, and William Morris. I know something about each of them but not sufficient to compare with one another.

But so far the list includes only men. Women have always suffered under social disadvantages and in earlier years they were even more onerous than now. Yet we all know from personal experience that women often have great strength and courage in the most difficult of circumstances. Among the most outstanding with whose contribution I have some familiarity are Annie Besant, Emma Paterson, Sylvia Pankhurst, Beatrice Webb, Mary Macarthur and Ellen Wilkinson. The name of Isabel Brown may be unfamiliar to a younger generation but her name deserves to be included for her life-long commitment to socialism and her outstanding work in support of Republican Spain in the late 1930s. Of contemporary figures a woman I very much admire is Alice Mahon MP. There are also any number of women who, unknown to recorded history have contributed so much to human progress.

There are also the rank-and-file stalwarts of the labour movement, men and women, who have served it unselfishly for many years, without any expectation of reward, other than have the satisfaction of contributing to the welfare of mankind. I remember too the many who gave their lives in the struggle against fascism, including the volunteers who fought in the International Brigade.

I finally decided to confine my choice to people who I have known or whose contribution is still of contemporary significance. Of the people who were alive during my lifetime, or are still alive, I would name four: Tony Benn and Jack Jones, who, fortunately, are still with us, and Tom Mann and G. D. H. Cole.

I include Tony Benn because of his consistent role as a tribune of the common people both inside and outside parliament and of his incomparable ability to win people for progressive causes; Jack Jones because of his life-long dedication to working people and his talented leadership in the trade union movement; Tom Mann, because he was a superb agitator among all working people, irrespective of their craft or occupation; and G. D. H. Cole, because he demonstrated, with immense scholarship, that the struggle for democracy, radicalism, the workers' movement and socialism are all part of a continuing and noble tradition in the struggle for the betterment of mankind.

This leaves two of an even earlier generation—both from the working class—whose ideas and influence need to be strengthened to this day. One of them, James Connolly, though born in Scotland, will forever be associated with the cause of Irish independence from British rule. He was also an internationalist and socialist. He demonstrated by his example and by his writings the progressive relationship between the anti-colonial struggle, internationalism and socialism. He was a towering giant of the labour movement but it it probably not appropriate to claim him as a Briton.

The second of this earlier generation, and my final choice, is Keir Hardie. He led the fight for an independent political party, based upon organised labour and committed to a socialist objective. He was well aware that such a party needed to address itself to the everyday interests of working people and should seek representation in every forum where it could have influence, including parliament and local authorities. He recognised that the struggle for independent parliamentary representation would form an integral part of a wider labour movement engaged in every kind of popular struggle against exploitation, colonialism and war. His example and ideas were an inspiration to us all.

***Jim Mortimer** is a well-known labour-movement activist and former general secretary of the Labour Party.*

Reviews

Books to be remembered (8)

Thomas Hodgkin, *Letters from Palestine, 1932–36* (ed. E.C. Hodgkin, London, 1986)

Thomas Hodgkin was born in 1910 into an upper middle-class family. One grandfather was a banker and the other the Master of Balliol. His father was a fellow, then a Provost of Queen's College, Oxford. Hodgkin himself went on a scholarship to Balliol. Hodgkin was from his early days interested in the Middle East, and after graduating he became an unpaid assistant to an archaeology group conducting excavations at Jericho. This was not to his central interests and in April 1934 he obtained a junior position in the administration of the government of Palestine.

Britain had been awarded the mandatory trusteeship of Palestine in the very early days of the League of Nations (1920). Already the Balfour Declaration of 1917 had encouraged the idea of a national home for the Jewish people in Palestine. Arab opposition was evident from the earliest days and there were bloody clashes already in 1910 and 1921. In 1929 there was a violent outbreak with a large number of deaths of both Jews and Arabs. Under the mandate Britain was theoretically obliged to safeguard the civil and religious rights of all nationalities within their control, but by the time Hodgkin entered the government service in the spring of 1934 no progress had been achieved on behalf of the Arab peoples. The Jewish population had risen from 55,000 in 1918 to around a quarter of a million in the early 1930s. By this time those Arabs living in Palestine were arguing for three major changes of policy: the end to Jewish immigration; the introduction of legislation to prohibit further sales of land by the Arabs to Jewish settlers; and the establishment of a responsible national government.

For all political purposes the British mandate was an autocracy over which the Arab population had no effective power, and the attempts to introduce safeguards over their rights has always failed. The letters collected in Hodgkin's *Letters from Palestine* were mostly written to members of the author's family and they provide an important historical document of this era. They are only occasionally directly political in character, but the dismay that Hodgkin was experiencing as a result of British rule is increasingly evident, and he was to retire from government service in the summer of 1936. When he returned to England he offered the marxist journal the *Labour Monthly* a detailed article on British rule. Reprinted in the volume under review, it was originally published in July 1936 and represents a statement of the first importance.[1] It should be noted that, as far as is known, Hodgkin was not a marxist when he first went to Palestine. It was not only his experiences there that moved him to the left, but also the general background of the mid-1930s in an increasingly troubled world.

The extent and depth of his political views were strikingly revealed in this article. It was a bitter criticism of the British administration of the mandate. He identified three main points, or what he called falsehoods. The first was that the unrest had no political justification; the second was that the disturbances were the result of deliberate instigation, especially from the outside world; and the third, that the British administration was 'gentle' in its repression of the unrest.

Hodgkin insisted that there were serious reasons for the existence of such widespread disturbances. He began by noting that the Palestine Arabs had been induced to desert the Turks during the last years of the 1914–18 war by promises of freedom, while 'for the last eighteen years [they] have endured an undiluted British autocracy'. There was no vestige of self-government and all the responsible political posts were held, not by the Palestinians, but by the British. There had been offers of a legislative council but always with British control in the last resort. Further, it was clear that once the Jews, who already controlled the economic life of Palestine and had a secure footing on the land, formed a numerical majority, they would become politically dominant. 'Then goodbye to any hopes of an independent Palestine.'

Hodgkin insisted that there were no foreign agents of any number and the unrest and the physical violence had the support of almost all sections of the Arab people. His strongest criticisms were of the repression which the administration exercised in vigorous physical terms. The government, he wrote, 'had shown itself at its most brutal in the military raids against the villages'. And he ended his article by the comparison between Italy's invasion of Abyssinia, then a major issue in international politics, and the political and administrative methods being employed by the British mandatory power.

This volume of letters and observations by Hodgkin should not be neglected by anybody concerned with the Israeli-Palestinian issue of our contemporary world. It is hardly a new understanding that the terrible tragedy of today has its beginnings in the years after 1918, but the historical background to the contemporary crisis can never be omitted from any analysis. While taking full note of the reprehensible acts of violence so often taken by the oppressed, we must recognise the long agonies of the Palestinian peoples, too seldom appreciated by the major powers. And the agonies continue…

John Saville

Note
1. British Resident, 'The events in Palestine', *Labour Monthly*, July 1936, pp.409–17; see also the same author's 'Is Palestine prosperous?', *Labour Monthly*, November 1936, pp.683–92.

Catherine Hall, Keith McClelland and Jane Rendall, *Defining the Victorian Nation: Class, Race, Gender and the British Reform Act of 1867* (Cambridge University Press, Cambridge, 2000), ISBN 0-521-57218-5, xiii+303pp., £45.00 hbk; ISBN 0-521-57653-9, £16.95, pbk.

Why did the Conservatives ally with right-wing Liberal rebels to defeat a moderate reform bill and then, having formed a minority government, allow their own measure—already regarded as so extreme that three cabinet ministers, including the astute future Marquis of Salisbury, resigned—to be radically transformed by left-wing amendments, thereby permitting in 1867 the enfranchisement of a significant proportion of the urban working class?

This set of paradoxical events attracted some outstanding historical writing in the 1960s. Maurice Cowling, described by *The Times* (12 September 2001) as 'our greatest living historian', provided in 1867: *Disraeli, Gladstone and Revolution* (1967) an account in terms of 'high politics', a term he was not until later to introduce into British historiography. By contrast, Royden Harrison, in his outstanding *Before the Socialists: Studies in Labour and Politics, 1861–1881* (1965), stressed the centrality of extra-parliamentary agitation and of what he called 'the "Rochdale" argument'—that since 1848 a respectable, prudent, moderate aristocracy of labour had become highly influential—although neither to the exclusion of parliamentary politics. A third monograph, F. B. Smith's fine *The Making of the Second Reform Bill* (1966), encompassed the differing emphases of Cowling and Harrison.

Since 1965–7, and in the absence of any further specialist research, it is Cowling's interpretation that has dominated the field. For example, even John Belchem contends:

> it was 'high politics' not extra-parliamentary pressure that prompted Disraeli to accept radical amendments which transformed the government bill into an extensive household suffrage measure...[1]

Harrison's work has regularly been misread, as by Eric J. Evans who rejects it as a 'heroically wrong-headed attempt to suggest that the second Reform Act was dictated by the ruling classes' perception of the "the proximity to revolutionary situations"...'(*The Forging of the Modern State: Early Industrial Britain, 1783–1870* (1983), p.346). In his introduction to the second edition of *Before the Socialists* Harrison reflects ruefully on his 'innocence' at not having expressed his argument more clearly (Gregg Revivals, Aldershot, 1994, p. xxxii).

This is a highly unsatisfactory situation and a new synthesis is desperately required, yet the authors of *Defining the Victorian Nation* do not attempt one. James Vernon, in an admiring review, considers that one of their agendas appears to be 'move beyond the tired old debates about the causes of the 1867 Reform Act: whether it was an unintended consequence of high-political manoeuvring and shifting parliamentary loyalties or a measured response to the popular political agitation for reform'.[2] At the very end of their text, however, there is explicit support for Harrison's argument when Catherine Hall mentions, almost incidentally, that:

> The electoral reform legislation went through after the second Hyde Park demonstration and debacle [of 6 May 1867] had finally convinced all but the most hard-line of the conservatives that a new settlement was inevitable (p.229).

Harrison argued, in a particularly subtle and convincing passage:

> In the 1860s the British working class exhibited certain 'contradictory' characteristics...it had attained precisely that level of development at which it was safe to concede its enfranchisement and dangerous to withhold it (*Before the Socialists*, p.133).

Hall cites a prime piece of evidence supporting this part of Harrison's case. In a speech in the Commons Edward Baines, Radical MP for Leeds, maintained:

92 Socialist History 25

> These are the men…who carry on the vast and varied industry of the country; they till your soil, they work your mines and machinery, they manufacture the products which command the markets of the world; their labour and skill make all your capital available, and produce all your comforts and luxuries; they navigate your ships of war and trade, and they fill the ranks of your armies. Their sinews are strong, their energies are not surpassed, their courage is high, their natural abilities are as good as those of the classes above them, they are now an educated people who daily read the news of all the world.

He concluded, Hall paraphrases: 'It was dangerous…to leave such men unrepresented' (p.227).

> The text is divided into four sections. The longest is a jointly written introduction. Keith McClelland's survey of the working-class movement is unchallenging though plausible, maintaining that after 1848 it underwent a 'masculinization' with the development of heavy industry: coalmining, engineering, the metal trades, iron shipbuilding. Jane Rendall's discussion of the campaign for female suffrage is easily the most original chapter, showing how women householders in the boroughs attempted to register themselves as electors in 1867–8, frequently successfully, alongside impressive petitioning for the appropriate extension of the Act of 1867. She points out that Helen Blackburn's *Women's Suffrage*, an account published by a participant in 1902, remains the principal history of this early movement. It is very much to be hoped that she is currently preparing its replacement. Finally Catherine Hall looks at the Jamaican 'Insurrection' of 1865 and, less convincingly, Fenianism. She ends with several engrossing pages on Parliament's agreeing to the dissolution of Jamaica's representative government, granted as early as 1662 (only seven years after its annexation by Britain) to the white planters who by the 1860s were fearful of the rising number of black members in the House of Assembly, and the island becoming instead a crown colony with a governor. There is no overall conclusion. In many respects the subject of this book was better handled in Hall's earlier article, 'Rethinking Imperial Histories: The Reform Act of 1867' (*New Left Review*, no. 208 [November/December 1994]), in which she wove the various themes together herself.

It is also a curiously slipshod volume. Thomas Woolner's 'Civilization', a sculpture of 1866 of a mother teaching her child the Lord's Prayer against a scene of ancient British cannibalism, discussed in the introduction though not elsewhere, is reproduced on the cover of the paperback edition I have for review. But what are hardback readers, whose libraries, like my own, discard the dustwrappers on accession, supposed to do? The 'Cast of characters', a useful appendix, omits the prime ministers, Russell and Derby, yet includes one individual, Daniel O'Donoghue, unmentioned in the text as well as the five members, also otherwise unmentioned, of the trade union 'Junta' which itself does not appear in the index. Most disturbing of all, Figure 2, 'Percentage of adult males over twenty-one enfranchised, 1861 and 1871', a diagram using percentages drawn from an article by K.Theodore Hoppen, so shuffles them around that *all* eighteen are wrong. The result is nonsense, but that has escaped the attention of three authors, the copy editor and anyone else who cast an eye over the proofs.

Notes
1. John Belchem, *Industrialization and the Working Class: The English Experience, 1750–1900* (1990), p.179.
2. *History Workshop Journal*, no.52 (Autumn 2001), p.261.

David Goodway
School of Continuing Education, University of Leeds

John Shepherd, *George Lansbury: At the Heart of Old Labour* (Oxford University Press, Oxford, 2002), ISBN 0-19-820164-8, 407pp., £35.00 hbk.

As *Socialist History* readers will no doubt be well aware, George Lansbury was one of the foremost pioneers of British socialism. Born to working class parents in Suffolk in 1859, Lansbury later became synonymous with the East End of London, where his parents had finally settled by the 1870s. Having met and married Bessie Brine, whose role in Lansbury's life was of crucial importance, Lansbury undertook an ill-fated journey to Australia in 1884, only to return to England and begin what was to be a prestigious political career.

Like many later Labour leaders, Lansbury's political life was first awakened to Gladstonian Liberalism, to which end he worked successfully as a Liberal agent from 1886. Even so, Christianity and an awareness of the acute poverty that surrounded him eventually forged in Lansbury a socialist worldview, leading him to help establish the Bow and Bromley branch of the Social Democratic Federation (SDF) in 1892. Over nearly ten years, Lansbury worked hard to help extend the SDF's influence across London and the country as a whole. To this effect, he served as an effective party organiser, and was elected to the board of guardians responsible for poor relief in Bow and Bromley. Though he failed to gain election to parliament in the 1890s, he nevertheless served as a borough councillor from 1893, campaigning among the unemployed and in support of women's suffrage. By 1901, however, Lansbury had joined the ILP, reaffirmed his Christianity, and sought to propagate his socialist beliefs through the newly established Labour Representation Committee, later Labour Party. Eventually, in December 1910, George Lansbury stood as a Labour candidate and was successfully elected to represent the people of Bow and Bromley in parliament.

Lansbury's first time in parliament proved to be an eventful if short-lived affair, as he sensationally resigned his seat in 1912 in opposition to the Liberal government's failure to enact universal suffrage. The following year, he was gaoled for incitement following a speech in support of Sylvia Pankhurst's WSPU. Though he did not return to the Commons until 1922, Lansbury remained a prominent Labour figure. Locally, he continued to champion the residents of Poplar; nationally, he helped establish and, from 1913, edit the *Daily Herald*. Throughout the Great War, Lansbury held true to his pacifist principles and opposed the conflict. He supported the Russian revolutions, remaining sympathetic to the Soviet Union and advocating communist affiliation to the Labour Party until the late 1920s. Throughout the post war decade, Lansbury was perhaps best known for leading the Poplar borough council in revolt against the London County Council and in support of the growing ranks of unemployed workers.

By the end of the 1920s, Lansbury had become a regular member of Labour's National Executive Committee, and although overlooked in the first Labour cabinet, was appointed First Commissioner of Works by MacDonald in 1929. He opposed the proposed cuts in unemployment benefit that contributed the fall of the government in 1931, emerging from the subsequent general election as the only Labour cabinet minister to retain his seat. Consequently, he became the leader of the parliamentary party and, from 1932, of the Labour Party generally. During this time, Lansbury did much to maintain the party's presence in the Commons, although he was famously forced to resign the leadership in 1935 as the party began to shift its policy in response to fascist aggression. As the TUC and many in the party began to contemplate a military response to fascism, Lansbury's pacifism stood at odds with the prevailing political mood. Nevertheless, he remained an advocate of peace and a tireless party worker until his death in 1940.

Obviously, such a whistle-stop tour through Lansbury's life does not do the man justice. Thankfully, John Shepherd's biography does so magnificently, detailing the causes, inspirations and connotations of Lansbury's commitment to the socialist cause. Shepherd combines his subject's achievements on the national stage with his dedication to both his family and the people of the East End, among whom he lived from childhood until his death. As Shepherd makes clear, Lansbury did not fit easily into the categories of either 'socialist intellectual' or 'trade unionist'. Certainly, he wrote extensively, not least for the *Daily Herald*. Yet Lansbury was a man of conviction rather than theory, and it is the consistency of his belief and action—shaped primarily by his Christian faith—that comes across most clearly in this biography. In many ways, his political trajectory was typical of his contemporaries, moving from Liberalism to socialism via the SDF, ILP and Labour Party. But Lansbury was above all an idealist, something Shepherd places at the basis of Lansbury's thought and action.

Crucially, Shepherd gives due attention to all periods of Lansbury's long and eventful life. During this time, he went from worker agitator to borough councillor to backbench rebel and eventually to Labour Party leader. Throughout, he remained loyal to his party and to the wider cause of socialism. At the same time, his idealism was sometimes a political weakness. Harold Laski famously accused Lansbury of having a 'bleeding heart that ran away with his bloody head', while Ernest Bevin more pointedly poured scorn on Lansbury's last days as Labour leader when he referred to his 'hawking' his conscience around the party in response to the Abyssinian crisis. Throughout the biography, Shepherd skilfully details the ways in which Lansbury was at times overtaken by political events and outmanoeuvred by opponents. Then as now, hardheaded pragmatism often won out against socialist idealism, although Lansbury's legacy appears only to benefit from his steadfast conviction.

On reading *George Lansbury*, it becomes clear that previous biographies of 'Good old George' have only scratched the surface of his long and eventful life. True, Shepherd's account is occasionally repetitive, but this is often due to its thoroughness. Although not quite a classic of the Pimlott on Dalton or Marquand on MacDonald mould, Shepherd's *George Lansbury* will no doubt become the definitive account of Lansbury's life for some time to come. It is a fitting testament to a central figure of the British labour and socialist movement.

Matthew Worley
University of Reading

Ahmad Alawad Sikainga, *'City of Steel and Fire': A Social History of Atbara, Sudan's Railway Town, 1906–1984* (James Curry, Oxford, 2003), ISBN 0-85-255962-3, 220pp., £17.95 pbk.

'City of Steel and Fire' is just one of the names bestowed on Atbara, the town in northern Sudan, which as the title of Sikainga's excellent study suggests, has become synonymous with the development of Sudan's railways. But the steel and fire of the title refers not just to the physical presence of the railway in Atbara, but more importantly to the fact that throughout the twentieth century it became one of the most important centres of working class politics in Sudan, both during the colonial period and in the period since formal independence from British rule. Atbara's prominence as a centre of political resistance is connected with the growth and development of the working class and particularly the railway workers of Atbara but also with the activities of the Sudanese Communist Party, which for much of the last century was the second largest communist party in Africa, and which fought to make the town a 'fortress of working people'. Sikainga's book is therefore an attempt to provide not only a social history of a town, its workers and an industry, but also a political and cultural history of the struggles of the workers and people of Atbara and the Sudan throughout the twentieth century.

Atbara, as Sikainga explains, had the largest concentration of industrial workers in the Sudan. It was the headquarters of the Sudan railways and the birthplace of the Sudanese labour movement. As such it was a town that played a major role in the anti-colonial struggle and which continued to play an important role in the struggles of the people of the Sudan against repressive regimes, both military and civilian, that usurped power in the post-colonial period. Indeed, as this book explains, Atbara and its people assumed such a central position in Sudanese politics, that the military government of Nimeiri took measures to crush the workers of Atbara and their organisations, such as the Sudan Railway Workers Union, even going as far as to effectively demolish the railway network in Sudan in the process. Nevertheless the railway workers of Atbara played a leading role in the events that led to the demise of Nimeiri's government in 1985, just as they had in the demise of the Abboud military regime in 1964. However, the repressive measures implemented by Nimeiri's regime were continued by the current National Islamic Front government, which has persecuted trade union leaders and dismissed thousands of railway workers.

Sikainga's study also seeks to provide a more general analysis of the role of labour in modern societies in Africa and the Middle East in which Islam is a powerful influence, as well as an analysis of the weaknesses exhibited in the struggles of the railway workers of Atbara and other parts of Sudan. It is perhaps in this regard that the book is at its weakest, largely because these are questions that require much more thorough examination than the author is able to provide, and which fit uneasily in a social and political history of the town of Atbara. There is for example very little consideration of the impact of external influences, particularly those exercised by the big powers on Sudan, both those that sought to prop up the neo-colonial regimes and those like the Soviet Union which exerted a strong influence on the Sudanese Communist Party.

'*City of Fire and Steel*' is based on extensive archival research and many interviews with workers, activists, trade union officials and others connected with the town of Atabara. It does manage to be both a social history of Atbara as well as a wider political history of the struggles of the town's railway workers and the labour movement in Sudan. In so doing it conveys something of the dignity of this remarkable town and its people and makes an important contribution to Sudanese history as well as to African labour history.

Hakim Adi
Middlesex University

Vladimir Mau and Irina Starodubrovskaya, *The Challenge of Revolution: Contemporary Russia in Historical Perspective* (Oxford University Press, Oxford, 2001), ISBN 0-19-924150-3, xii+369pp., £50.00 hbk.

When Louis XVI was told of the storming of the Bastille he is said to have asked: 'C'est une révolte?' To which the Duc de la Rochefoucauld-Liancourt replied: 'Non, Sire, c'est une révolution.' In more than two centuries since then there has been much uncertainty and dispute over what actually is a revolution. In their well researched and contentious new book Mau and Starodubrovskaya, younger Russian scholars and 'radical' political activists, recognise at the outset that the concept of revolution is 'very nebulous' (p.9). Hence whether a given historical event or process is so classified or not depends on how one defines the term. It necessarily entails a certain measure of arbitrariness.

The overturn of the old order in England in the 1640s, France in 1789–94, and Russia from February 1917 are generally recognised, as they are by Mau and Starodubrovskaya, to have been revolutions changing the course of history. Much more disputable is their characterisation of the limited period of *perestroika* in the late 1980s and early 1990s as 'full-blown revolution' comparable to the classical revolutions just referred to (p.183). There is perhaps an element of subjectivity here in so far as this was a period in which the authors were themselves actively involved. This description of perestroika as a revolution was initiated by Gorbachev on 3 July 1986 (rather than the next year, as the authors write in their preface—p.vii.) It flowed no doubt from a desire to boost the importance of, and support for, his progressive reform policies rather than from a scientific analysis of the question. The latter would surely require attention as to whether or not such changes were solidly grounded enough to assert themselves in one form or another over a substantial period. (In this I would agree with the authors in their treatment of the February and October revolutions of 1917 as 'phases of one revolution'—p.183.) In fact so unclear and unsubstantial are the shapes of what our authors call the 'current Russian revolution' that they acknowledge that its outcome is virtually unforeseeable' (p.332).

What then is a revolution? One can join with the authors in rejecting the widespread definition of revolution as violence. Like them one can see it as entailing a 'transformation of society' which occurs particularly 'with an enfeebled state that is unable to control the events and changes taking place'. However their designation of this as occurring 'spontaneously' (p.328) is not necessarily correct. Thus in Russia in 1917 you had a combination of spontaneous mass discontent and conscious political leadership and direction given by Lenin and the Bolshevik party. Elsewhere the authors sensibly weaken the iron role that they elsewhere seem to be ascribing to spontaneity. Thus they write more correctly of revolution as 'an objective and *mainly* spontaneous process' with the leaders able to have 'a substantial influence' on the form of that process' (p.179, emphasis added).

Mau and Starodubrovskaya have discarded much, though not all, of the Marxist outlook, which in its Soviet form had been that of the bulk of Russian intellectuals. This is most strikingly evident in their rejection of class antagonisms, which for Marxism is the core element in revolutions. This was expressed very clearly by Lenin when he wrote in 1917: 'The passing of state power from one class to another is the first, the principal, the basic sign of a *revolution*, both in the strictly scientific and in the practical political meaning of that term' (LCW, 24, p.44. Emphasis in original.)

Although well aware of the social antagonisms that fuel revolutionary movements, the authors seek to distinguish their present views from Marxism. They insist: 'A class analysis the basis of Marxist approaches...is not applicable to revolution. In conditions of social fragmentation the basic element of the social structure is a much smaller unit than a class' (p.334). Hence to classes they counterpose polarised groups, strata or forces as though these forms of social organisation were not complementary to classes rather than exclusive of them. In fact, the redistribution of property, to which the authors rightly attach importance, was a big class issue in the French and Russian revolutions. In Russia in 1917 it was championed by three All-Russian Congresses of Peasant Soviets. They supported their own party, the Socialist Revolutionaries (SRs), which had been formed at the beginning of the century. With associated national and peasant parties, the SRs obtained an absolute majority (56.9 per cent) of the forty-four-and-a-half million votes cast in November 1917 for the Constituent Assembly. In those elections the Bolsheviks, with 24 per cent of the total poll, received an absolute majority of the working class vote on the basis of an uncompromising proletarian class appeal.

Despite their criticisms of Marxism and their rejection of socialist politics, Mau and Starodubrovskaya paradoxically identify themselves with Marx's historical method, quoting approvingly and at length from Marx's *Capital*. They signify their agreement with their friend and colleague Egor Gaidar when he wrote: 'Economic materialism remains a powerful tool of analysis and prediction.' This, he said, was in no way altered by the collapse of the 'socialist experiment linked to the name of its founder' (p.325).

Among a wide variety of questions which are discussed is whether the 'so-called fascist revolutions', which are examined mainly in their German Nazi form, should be seen as revolutions or counter-revolutions. The authors do not seem to have made up their minds about this. This is not due to some sort of sneaking sympathy for Hitler, Mussolini et al., but, I believe, results from their mistaken rejection of class criteria in evaluating fascism (which is not the same as suggesting that they should have reduced all aspects of fascism to purely class criteria).

An interesting feature of the book is its interviews with Gorbachev and three other prominent leaders from the perestroyka period (Yakovlev, Burbulis and Gaidar).

Considerable informed attention is given to economic questions by the book's two economist authors. They see them as central to the 'economic cycle of revolution', which is a term that they use interchangeably with 'economic crisis of the revolution'. They explain that what they have in mind is that always 'revolution is accompanied by economic crisis, which develops in a cyclical form. The economic situation deteriorates as the revolution deepens, and stabilises as the country emerges from revolution' (p.192) The tables and figures which they provide are very useful as an empirical basis for their 'distinctive' (p.333) and controversial theory of revolution. However the authors' aim of showing how this 'can help us to understand what is taking place in Russia' (p.326) can hardly be deemed to have been realised when they conclude, with commendable frankness, that 'the outcome of the revolution [in Russia] is virtually impossible to predict' (p.332). One can only hope that they will be proved wrong in their suggestion that in their country 'conditions for a post-revolutionary dictatorship' were 'ripening', although forecasting that this 'would take a fairly mild form and would soon come to nothing' (p.338).

As 'free-market radicals', Mau and Starodubrovskaya disdain the steps, now rescinded, taken under Gorbachev for industrial self-management with election of factory directors by the workers. They write that the development of such democracy was 'incompatible with carrying out any responsible macroeconomic policy' (p.235–6). This approach is, of course, a capitalist one entailing an extension of 'private property, setting of prices by the free market and market competition' championed as 'vitally important for Russia' (p.245).

There is much for socialists to be critical about in this book. However there is also much that is interesting and challenging in the use made of the wide range of sources listed in its 21-page bibliography. They suggest important lines of research which it is to be hoped will be debated and extended in the years ahead both in Britain and in Russia, where the book has been published in its original Russian under the title *Great Revolutions from Cromwell to Putin*.

Monty Johnstone
Monty Johnstone is an editorial adviser to Socialist History

Bob Jessop, *The Future of the Capitalist State* (Polity Press, Cambridge, 2002), ISBN 0-74-562273-9, 344pp, £17.99 pbk.

Bob Jessop has spent the greater part of his academic life engaged with state theory. In this book he has produced a complex tautology which will be of interest to scholars concerned with a wide range of theoretical problems which bear on the question of the state in capitalist societies. For the primary aim is to elaborate the theoretical foundations for a research agenda on the capitalist type of state in contemporary capitalism, focusing on its economic and social policy. Jessop defines the state as a relatively unified ensemble of socially embedded, socially regularised, and strategically selective institutions, organisations, social forces, and activities organised around (or at least involved in) making collectively binding decisions for an imagined political community. He assumes the inherent improbability of stable capital accumulation based solely on market forces and sees the state apparatus and state power as critical factors in shaping the dynamic of accumulation as well as being shaped in their turn by that dynamic. But he doesn't regard the state as fully determined by the logic of capitalism and he rejects the idea of determination in the last instance by the economic. He sees that the necessary institutional separation of the state from the market economy permits an operational autonomy which cannot guarantee that it serves the needs of capital. He also uses a broader definition of the economic than is usual in the economics profession, conceptualises the economy as co-constituted by extra-economic factors and finds limits to economic determination in resistances from a wide range of social forces. Jessop argues for the primacy of production in the overall circuit of capital, but only as an ecological dominance—always contingent and historically variable, mediated in and through the operational logic of other systems—nevertheless able to imprint its developmental logic on those other systems more than they can impose their logic on it. Globalisation, in this view, enhances the dominance of capital, if only temporarily, by expanding the scope for accumulation to escape the constraints of the other systems (such as the state system) in the ecology of capitalism.

This framework draws on the regulation approach to political economy, as well as the work of Poulantzas and Gramsci and critical discourse analysis. Thus capitalism is conceived as an accumulation regime and a mode of social regulation, the state is understood as a social relation rather than a subject, though intellectuals are said to have a prominent role in the exercise of hegemony and the construction of an historic bloc. Discourse is central to the way these are imagined. The state is responsible for securing the conditions for capital accumulation and the reproduction of labour-power, as well as maintaining social cohesion. But it can do this by a variety of modes of regulation and patterns of governance. Institutions matter and their forms are irreducible to the categories of the capital relation. There is, moreover, no single best solution, much less a perfect fit which fully integrates the market economy in a market society. The boundaries between the state and civil society are discursively constituted, essentially contested and liable to change.

Much of the book focuses on what Jessop calls the Keynesian Welfare National State (KWNS) and the uncertain transition from the KWNS to the Schumpeterian Competition State as the system of Atlantic Fordism began to disintegrate in the period since 1970. The reader will see that this schema depends on the explanatory utility of numerous theories which Jessop imports into his analysis as it develops. Many of these—such as Fordism, post-Fordism, capitalist regulation theory, globalisation, the Schumpeterian competition state etc—involve contested assumptions which Jessop himself occasionally interrogates and inflects. Properly understanding the work in question demands expertise in a broad range of disciplines and specialisms. But the complexity of Jessop's stylised model goes beyond such considerations as he simultaneously seeks to avoid simple causal relationships while embracing as many independent variables within his theory as each of his conceptual categories will stand. He allows, for example, that distinct national variants of the KWNS evolved and proceeds to list six types of economic and social intervention corresponding to them. In terms of governance he also distinguishes a further four types corresponding to four ways of governing the division of labour. More concrete analyses, he allows, might want to examine secondary variations of the KWNS arising from their internal articulation, social bases, gendered inflection, degree of family-friendliness and so on. All of this is made even more complex by the recognition that changes in the KWNS were related to an evolving division of labour in Atlantic Fordism and the wider international economy and to different patterns of competitive advantage. But, for all these variations, he insists on their basic congruence at his more abstract-simple levels of analysis. The system thus theorised is said to have helped secure the conditions for Fordist economic expansion during the years of the long boom, while Fordist economic expansion is also said to have helped secure the conditions for expansion of the KWNS. This system is the one that entered a crisis in the 1970s and 1980s. The causes, according to Jessop, were inevitably multiple and complex, including stagflationary, fiscal-financial, political, social, demographic (and so on)—some secular and structural in character, others merely conjunctural.

In the course of this multi-level crisis the social wage was discursively transformed from a functional support of capitalism to a cost of international production. Jessop has quite a lot to say about the discursive mediation of crisis and the conditions of its success. But for the most part he simply adopts the narrative which became fashionable in the 1980s in certain countries—notably the USA and the UK. This is the story of the 'competition state', the knowledge economy, flexible production, informationalism, etc. Forgetting for a moment the need to cover all bases—a procedure which has already produced a multitude of independent variables and an accompanying array of theories—Jessop tells us that the knowledge-based economy appears to have a genuine potential to initiate a new long wave of economic expansion. For once there is no theoretical cover worth invoking for this surprising assertion. Long waves of capitalist development remain an unexplained pattern rather than something we understand. Forecasts, of course, have a nakedness about them which is not true of system-building in a historical context, the method which generally characterises works of this sort. Instead dense clusters of complex relationships are manufactured. Globalisation, for example, in Jessop's reading of it, denotes a supercomplex series of multicentric, multiscalar, multitemporal, multiform and multi-causal processes. This definition rules out its use as a unitary causal mechanism. But that doesn't stop the author from assuming that it contributes in however mediated and indirect a way to the structural integration and strategic coordination of the capitalist economy on a global scale. But it is difficult to see how this could ever be established in any scientific way. The same is true of this work in its totality. In trying to establish the theoretical foundations for a research agenda on the capitalist state Jessop has certainly crafted an ingenious schema; the space allowed here enables me to mention only the half of it. It will require many times the ingenuity to make it useful as a method of concrete analysis of any particular state in any particular conjuncture.

John Callaghan
University of Wolverhampton

Andy Croft, *Comrade Heart: A Life of Randall Swingler* (Manchester, Manchester University Press, 2003), ISBN 0-7190-6334-5, 320pp., £45.00 hbk.

Andy Croft's biography of Randall Swingler discloses the life and work of a poet, writer, political activist and war hero— an extraordinary and complex man. Born into a wealthy, well-connected Anglican family, the godson of the Archbishop of Canterbury, Swingler's early life was full of promise. Although brought up within strict religious parameters, reinforced by the guilt of sin, the large self-contained family enjoyed a cultured and privileged lifestyle. At preparatory school and Winchester college, which he attended from 1922, Swingler was successful, happy and confident. His warmth, humour and sharp intellect attracted his fellow pupils; he excelled at sports and his poetry was published in the school magazine. However, Croft interestingly identifies the development of a contradictory character; a sensitive, romantic nature coupled with a tendency towards asceticism that caused him to welcome suffering as proof of personal worth.

During his time at New College, Oxford, he was part of the 'charmed circle' of idealistic young men who provided the institution's intellectual leadership. Friends included Stephen Spender, Gabriel Carritt, Louis MacNeice and Dick Crossman, with whom he was particularly close. They explored the ideas of Marx, Lenin and Freud and Swingler briefly flirted with radical religious teachings. By this time, he was involved in so many activities that his studies began to suffer. Crossman, who was perhaps a steadying influence, moved to Germany in 1930 and in 1931, while Swingler met and fell in love with Geraldine Peppin, a talented pianist. Croft sees this year as a turning point for Swingler, when he suffered an emotional crisis that caused him to reconsider his values. He married Geraldine in the spring of 1933, dedicating his first published book of poetry, a collection of love poems, to her. However, much of his poetry now had a political message, their circle included many radicals and communists and this was the time Swingler made the defining decision to join the Communist Party.

As the Popular Front blossomed, his political views strengthened—the Spanish Civil War providing proof of the validity of his course—and this was expressed in his work. *The Times Literary Supplement* remarked that Swingler was an artist first, his politics coming 'a bad second', but he believed that all art is revolutionary, an expression of the people's needs, and perceived this to be under attack from fascism, capitalism and imperialism. He worked with Alan Bush to widen access to music and provided support to working-class writers and poets, contributed to the CP's Writers Group, the Unity Theatre, Left Book Club, For Intellectual Liberty and other Popular Front activities. By the late 1930s Swingler was writing regular reviews for the *Daily Worker*, editing *New Left Review* and establishing Fore Publications with part of his inheritance. *Our Time*, the magazine he launched and co-edited with poet and critic Edgell Rickword, was particularly influential during the war years. Although the publication was not owned by the CP, it was distributed through the network of party-owned bookshops and was subject to its vetting procedures.

The threat of war in Europe helped to build the Popular Front, but the Soviet—German Pact and the CPGB's acceptance of the CPSU's 'imperialist war' stance left communists isolated and confused. Like many of his comrades, Swingler repressed his private doubts to back the party line, attacking contemporaries who refused to do likewise for abandoning the true role of the artist. Not that the party's marginalised position prevented him from enjoying and participating fully in communist campaigns, as Croft records—suggesting again his tendency towards personal self-sacrifice. Nevertheless, when the communist movement swung behind the war effort following Hitler' invasion of the Soviet Union, it was a great relief for Swingler, who faced the hardships of military action with the uncompromising courage that had endeared him to his fellows during his student years. He was awarded the Military Medal for bravery in the field of battle and the book traces a growing tendency towards morbidity in his later art to a wartime experience which included being buried alive during action in Italy and emerging as the only survivor of his unit. War experiences also served to strengthen a detachment from his class, nurturing a hatred of the public school educated officer class, the inequalities and the need for unquestioning obedience. He refused to apply for a commission and his life among the ranks appears to have been one of shared friendship and understanding.

The camaraderie among the lower ranks—including prisoners of war—encouraged an optimistic belief that the post-war world would be one built on socialist principles. But these hopes soon shrank as the Cold War developed and political disappointment was made all the harder to bear because of a corresponding deterioration in his personal relationships. A rejection of the concept of ownership had led the Swinglers to pursue an 'open' marriage, a decision that caused Geraldine some grief, but during his wartime suffering she had become the focal point of his longings for normality and civilisation. As he planned a settled, monogamous lifestyle, Geraldine grew more successful and confident and her desire for independence grew. Disappointment marked his creative efforts too; a representative collection of his poetry, *The Years of Anger*, received little recognition as critics looked to new talents and fresh ideas. Efforts to establish the radical literary magazines *Arena* and *Circus* also foundered.

Shattered, rejected and sidelined—his financial situation increasingly precarious—Swingler began to drink heavily. Croft vividly sets him in a 'no man's land', between the mainstream and a party whose hierarchy now regarded its intellectuals with suspicion. A continuing disillusionment with communism, fuelled by what he saw as the British leadership's adherence to the Stalinist line, led him to leave the party in 1956. A last hope that the revelations of the CPSU's twentieth congress would bring immediate and sweeping change was dashed. *The Map*, which he wrote in 1966, revealed his distance from his earlier political passion—a work that sees humans as unimportant in the universe and the individual consciousness as a delusion, concluding that human-centred ideologies are a fallacy.

Swingler's final years were spent in virtual retreat in Essex, caring for his young son while Geraldine worked in London. The years of despair and disappointment, the smoking and drinking, began to take their toll on his health. Towards the end of his life, however, he experienced a kind of epiphany when he met his daughter Deborah—the result of a brief affair with Penelope Dimont in 1947. The effect of this new relationship on his volatile emotional state pushed him into euphoria. Perhaps it offered an opportunity to recompense for his desertion of her, to rectify one of the perceived failures of his life? Ironically, at the age of fifty-eight, he suffered a heart attack and died during one of his visits to Deborah, as they strolled through his old stomping ground around the communist party offices in London. His passing attracted little comment, a quiet family funeral, obituaries in *The Times* and *Daily Worker*.

We should be grateful to Andy Croft for rescuing the life and work of a lost literary hero—admirable in many ways but also flawed by a polemical nature that, at one extreme, nurtured a self-destructive admiration of martyrdom. Swingler's friend and fellow communist, Louis MacNeice, wrote of the appeal of the communist party that it 'demanded sacrifice' and Swingler was willing to sacrifice the opportunity to be a leading poet of his generation to the cause of human advancement. In this book the facts of Swingler's life are intertwined with his poetry, adding depth to Croft's analysis of his character and state of mind, and telling the fascinating story of his time.

Jean Jones
Jean Jones has written on the CPGB including SHS Occasional Papers on Ben Bradley and the League Against Imperialism

Matthew Worley, *Class against Class: The Communist Party in Britain Between the Wars* (I.B. Tauris, London, 2002) ISBN 1-86064-747-2, x+352pp., £37.50, hbk.

Matthew Worley is to be congratulated. His is the first book to deal with the Communist Party of Great Britain during its Class Against Class phase. Most historians of British communism have largely ignored this period from 1928 until 1933. Those that have dealt with it have done so in a cursory and condemnatory way. Both marxist and non-marxist historians have been of one accord, that the Class Against Class, or 'New Line', strategy was a complete disaster imposed on reluctant British communists by an all-powerful Communist International. Even communist writers have been unanimous in the view that the period offered little solace for the party and that in the short period that the policy was in operation party membership slumped and lethargy abounded.

In this well-researched and readable book, Worley takes issue with those who see the new line solely as an imposition by Moscow. The author argues that there were internal domestic reasons for the change of line that also played a part. Chief among these was the widespread disillusionment felt by communists in the wake of the defeat of the 1926 General Strike. Attitudes hardened against those who, in the communists' view, had betrayed the miners, including not just the leaderships of Labour Party and TUC but the rank and file as well. After 1926 communists were less inclined to view the Labour Party as a kindred spirit, and if it had not yet become another 'bourgeois party', a view that dominated the Class Against Class years, the signs were there that this would soon be the case. Another factor in pushing the communists into a reassessment of their previous united front strategy was the retaliatory measures taken against them in the trade union movement. Trades Councils too did not escape the crackdown on communists, and in 1927 the TUC threatened to withdraw recognition from any trades council that was either affiliated to or associated with the Minority Movement.

Matthew Worley outlines very well these internal developments that helped shaped British communists rejection of the united front policy that had prevailed since the party's formation in 1920–1. He also deals in some detail with the interventions by the Communist International (CI), particularly during the period of transition to the new line. The CI had first made known that a change of policy was desirable in a letter sent to the CPGB's Ninth Congress in October 1927. After that, there were constant comings and goings between Moscow and London as the party leadership reassessed its strategy after some considerable prodding by the CI. By the time of the CPGB's eleventh congress in December 1929, British communists had completely embraced the new strategy and had elected a party leadership that was fully in accord with the ideas of Class Against Class.

The character of these ideas and how they differed from previous communist practice is discussed by Worley in the last part of his book. One of the achievements of the strategy he describes was the emergence of a distinct communist culture. Through organisations like the British Workers' Sports Federation and the emerging local workers' theatre groups, communists managed to involve many workers in cultural and sporting pursuits. Among the lasting achievements of the BWSF was the mass trespass on Kinder Scout in the Peak District at which six members of the Manchester Young Communist League were arrested. He also describes the radical changes in communist policy towards the unions and the attempts establish new revolutionary unions freed from bureaucracy and right wing control. This only provided possible in two instances: amongst clothing workers, mainly based in London, and amongst some sections of Scottish miners. In both cases the experiments were short lived and the two red unions either collapsed or were merged.

All this and more Worley documents well. The book does have failings but these are overshadowed by its refreshingly novel approach of not seeing the CPGB merely as a plaything of Moscow. What then are the book's drawbacks? First and foremost, it only deals with part of the period. The Class Against Class policy was not finally jettisoned until the seventh congress of the Comintern in 1935. There is no doubt that its slow death started with Hitler's accession to power in February 1933 but it took almost two years before the united front become accepted communist strategy. In Britain, the CPGB did not finally urge its supporters to vote Labour, in the absence of a communist candidate, until the borough council elections of November 1934, and Worley, who effectively ends his narrative in 1931, ignores this interesting period in the later life of the new line.

Another disappointment is that so little attention is paid to the *Daily Worker*, which was finally founded in 1930 as a direct product of the new line. Under its editor Bill Rust it enthusiastically carried the party's strategy to an increasing number of workers and despite continual police harassment, fines, and the imprisonment of its staff, by the end of the period the paper was well established with a weekend readership of 50,000. Also missing, although acknowledged by Worley, is the party's almost lone campaign during the period against colonialism and racism. Communists, although small in number, fought an uphill battle in the labour movement to focus attention on the plight of colonial workers and their struggle for liberation. Such was their commitment that it resulted in leading party member Ben Bradley being sent to India where he was imprisoned with his Indian comrades after the famous Meerut Trial. At home, where white supremacist ideas were endemic, the communists fought hard against any attempts at what they saw as attempts to split the working class. The *Daily Worker* exposed racism in sport, particularly boxing and was instrumental in orchestrating a campaign on behalf of mixed-race children in Liverpool. In addition its daily anti-racist message did much to wean militant workers away from the ideas of Empire and Britain's right to rule.

Finally, one question which Worley does not answer, and nor for that matter do any other commentators on the period, is what would have happened if the CI had made no suggestions about the British party changing its strategy. Although a 'what if' question, we have strong indications of the answer in the decisions of the CPGB's ninth congress in October 1927, whose importance is ignored by most commentators, and, surprisingly, by Worley himself. Though a telegram was sent to the congress from Moscow informing delegates that it was necessary to adopt a harder line towards the Labour Party, this instruction did not arrive in time, and yet the congress delegates nevertheless agreed that in future communists would stand in opposition to Labour candidates at parliamentary elections. Once taken, this decision effectively ended the communists' campaign for affiliation to the Labour Party, which had been the cornerstone of the party's strategy since its formation. Whatever interventions Moscow may have made subsequently, the door to Class Against Class had already been opened.

These omissions and points of disagreement do not detract from the value of this work, which broadens our knowledge and increases our depth of understanding as to why British communists reacted the way they did in the face of a Labour Party moving steadily to the right. I wonder if there are any parallels today?

Mike Squires
Mike Squires is a historian of the CPGB and the biographer of Shapurji Saklatvala

Kevin Passmore (ed.), *Women, Gender and Fascism in Europe, 1919–45* (Manchester University Press, Manchester, 2003) ISBN 0-71906-617-4, 275pp., £14.99 pbk.

Any up-and-coming academic who aspires to produce a book based on conference papers destined to have a significant impact on several disciplines at once—and help establish his or her department as a centre of excellence—would do well to take a leaf out of Kevin Passmore's. First, he went to considerable trouble to plan the two-day conference 'Women, gender and the extreme right, 1919–1945' held in Cardiff in July 2001 with a judicious blend of ambition and pragmatism so that it attracted contributions from top experts on a wide range of Western and Eastern European countries, whether based in Europe or the USA. He then ensured that the diverse essays would acquire a cohesion rare in multi-author volumes by imposing a common format and set of issues to be addressed in each paper presented and hence in the resulting chapter. Third, he secured grants from funding bodies to help finance a project that involved onerous travel and accommodation costs that could not all be borne by the participants. Fourth, at an early stage rather than as an afterthought he secured the commitment of a major academic publisher to publish the proceedings in an affordable, attractively produced paperback. Fifth, he showed his personal commitment to the undertaking in the extensive editorial work required 'behind the scenes' to bring the twelve essays to a high level of cogency and fluency despite the fact that several of the authors are not native speakers or writers of English.

Finally, Passmore underwrote the coherence of the whole project by providing an introduction setting out the book's agenda followed up in a final synoptic essay in which he deftly draws on the rich empirical, and often highly original material presented in the individual case-studies to formulate answers to the questions posed at the outset. The result is that rarity of rarities, an academic book that does not fall short of the publisher's hype on the cover, but actually exceeds the expectations it raises. Inevitably, authors of such different backgrounds display uneven awareness of and interest in the wider issues raised by the complex nexus between the authoritarian right, fascism, and gender politics. Nevertheless, cumulatively, the book succeeds in making a significant contribution to women's history in relation to inter-war right-wing regimes, and to our understanding not just of how women can be exploited to fulfil patriarchal goals but in particular how historical circumstances can cause them to enter deep relationships of collusion and co-dependency with the extreme right of their own volition. Its particular strength lies in the way the dense empirical reconstruction of the case studies are framed within the editor's sophisticated heuristic framework to probe the complex and paradoxical relationships between women's emancipation and right-wing repression that emerged in inter-war Europe, and, I would add, are a feature of Western modernity as a whole.

One of the book's more refreshing aspects is that it is genuinely European (and not just Western European) in its scope, with essays on Italy, France, Germany, and Spain (both excellent), and on Romania, Serbia, Croatia, Hungary, Latvia and Poland. Moreover, the last three countries are covered by scholars educated in those countries, thereby suggesting that the accession of former East-bloc countries to academic Eurolandia will become a reality long before their full economic integration (the chapters on Latvia, Serbia and Croatia, are particularly good). It announces the advent of a new era in the study of extremism and gender in other respects too, namely by treating both components with a rare sense of taxonomic sophistication. Passmore has already made valuable contributions to comparative fascist studies, and thus displays a sensitivity—all too rare in an earlier generation of scholars—to the distinction that needs to be drawn between fascism and conservatism, even when that conservatism was not only modernised but partially fascistised as well, as in Spain, France, Hungary, Latvia, and Serbia. It is also heartening to find fascism no longer being routinely equated with reaction, counter-revolution, and the reinstatement of patriarchal gender stereotypes, but pursuing an agenda which subordinated the family to the interests of 'remaking the nation' in a totalising spirit that involved 'the defeat of ethnic, socialist and feminist enemies', and could also involve eugenic programmes anathema to traditional religious conservatives. In this respect the book is a valuable contribution to what has been controversially termed the 'new consensus' in fascist studies, the main theme of which is the cleavage between conservative reaction to liberalism and communism and fascism's revolutionary goal of the regenerated national community.

Perhaps the most valuable aspect of this book from a socialist perspective is the way it shatters the simplistic equation of feminist radicalism with the progressive left and fanatical fascism with a reactionary crusade against women, thus providing a salutary prophylactic to the Manichean mindset that can inform analyses on the book's topic even among academics who should know better. Certainly fascism is confirmed as intrinsically anti-feminist, because of its subordination of any notion of universal women's rights to the primacy of the reborn nation; however, it is also clear from the abundant empirical data the dozen chapters supply that in several countries some women, including some feminists, sincerely looked to fascism to empower them in a way that neither the communism nor the liberalism of the day could or would. It also emerges that in all the countries considered women could on occasions achieve unprecedented social mobility and political clout through accommodation with the extreme right, as long as they did not challenge the axiom of their 'natural' subordination to men in the political hierarchy or the public sphere. Women's collusion with fascism was thus far more than a simple case of patriarchal coercion or totalitarian indoctrination, but involved instead the ability of some women to find (an illusory?) fulfilment in the conjoining of their personal destiny with that of the nation, even if it could mean, as in the case of Nazism, sacrificing entire categories of their sisters who had been officially stigmatised as enemies of the national cause.

This leads to Passmore's penetrating insight that 'binary oppositions—traditional/modern, radical/reactionary, victim/victimiser—usually used to understand the extreme right must be rethought. Extreme right wing movements, like the right more generally, are not simply binary opposites of the left'. He concedes that 'It might crush the political representatives of the left—that is why the extreme right is extreme', but stresses that 'it also engages in dialogue with the left, modifying its own discourse to anticipate the reactions of, and win over, those it opposes'. It is this ambivalence and capacity for synthesis that 'enables fascism to 'include[s] groups which are assumed (rightly or wrongly) to be "normally" represented by the left—workers' and women's groups, for example' (p.267). Had the German revolutionary left understood this simple fact about Nazism when the Weimar Republic was in a state of terminal collapse it might have avoided wasting its ideological resources on attacking the 'social fascism' of the SPD and realised the inroads that Nazism was making into its own ideological heartland. Armed with this empirically founded realisation a generation of scholars influenced by post-war leftist feminism may have avoided squandering valuable research time on using fascist studies to conduct a thinly disguised crusade against right-wing patriarchy, and been less disconcerted at finding members of their gender, some of them highly articulate spokeswomen of the suffragette or feminist movements of the early twentieth century, sleeping figuratively and even literally with the enemy.

If this book has a weakness it is that it does not fully deliver on its title's promise to investigate 'gender' under fascism and the far right. Perhaps Passmore could be persuaded to organise another conference, this time exploring in depth, through an equally rich variety of case-studies, how European (and North American?) men coming of age in the inter-war period were discriminated against both in the official gender politics of fascist movements and conservative regimes thanks to their deeply engrained stereotypes about their innate gender roles. Under the Third Reich men were liable to persecuted, interned and murdered by the regime on eugenic, racial, or ideological grounds, if they did not fit the iconic image of the heroic, fecund, athletic, Aryan warrior male, unperturbed by any 'fuzzy boundaries' or self-doubt in his sense of the duties that nature had ordained him to fulfil both on the stage of history, and off stage in the work-place and the home in the service of the reborn nation. One day it might come to be more widely acknowledged that in most societies gender-stereotypes have always tended to act as a socially constructed bed of Procustus, and under extreme-right regimes men just as much as women were ruthlessly tailored to its size. Then at last we could begin to move beyond the crude binary opposition that pits patriarchal oppression against feminist emancipation, and realise that women are not the only victims of institutionalised male chauvinism in interwar Europe.

Roger Griffin
Professor in Modern History at Oxford Brookes University

Neville Kirk, *Comrades and Cousins: Globalization, Workers and Labour Movements in Britain, the USA and Australia from the 1880s to 1914* (Merlin Press, London, 2003), ISBN 0-850-365-155, x+224pp., £14.95 pbk.

This is an ambitious book. Spurred on by his interest in the contemporary process of globalisation, Neville Kirk takes as his starting point Ellen Wood's contention that 'globalization is not a new epoch but a long-term process, not a new kind of capitalism but the logic of capitalism as it has been from the start'. *Comrades and Cousins* represents his contribution to the study of that process. Accordingly, one of his general aims in writing the book 'is to plead the case for paying more attention than is commonly the case in the literature to the transatlantic, colonial and imperial dimensions of the history of workers and organised labour'. His other, more specific, purpose is to explore late nineteenth and early twentieth century developments at what he describes as 'the cross-national comparative level'. This involves, he explains, the consideration of 'discrete, but closely related aspects of workers' and labour movements' politics and ideologies—embracing, *inter alia*, questions of class, race, nation and empire—in Britain, the USA and Australia'.

It is a formidable agenda. However, *Comrades and Cousins* it is not quite as ambitious as it appears. Comparative history, of course, is exceptionally difficult to carry out with the appropriate combination of sensitivity, awareness and control. In fact, Kirk makes no claim to employing a tightly circumscribed methodology, whereby chronological boundaries, key developments and explanatory variables are carefully identified, strictly measured and scrupulously compared. The book consists, rather, in the author's own words, of three 'essays' on three different parts of the English-speaking world.

The first essay, 'Transatlantic Connections and American "Peculiarities": Labour Politics in the United States and Britain, 1893–1908', compares the politics of mainstream labour movements on either side of the Atlantic. Immersing himself in the labour press, the published papers of Samuel Gompers and the records of the American Federation of Labor and material from the (British) Trades Union Congress and Labour Party, Kirk examines, *inter alia*, how far American activists looked to the British experience, and the extent to which labour policies in the two countries converged. The second essay, 'The Australian "Workingman's Paradise" in Comparative Perspective, 1890-1914', by far the longest of the three, explores further the issue of national 'peculiarities'. Employing a more disparate range of sources, Kirk finds, not surprisingly perhaps, that Australia was commonly perceived, by activists and others, to offer working people a much wider range of opportunities than was available to them in the 'Old World'. The third essay, 'The Rule of Class and the Power of Race: Socialist Attitudes to Class, Race and Empire during the "Era of New Imperialism", 1899-1910', draws upon British publications such as the *Clarion*, the *Labour Leader* and the *British Citizen and Empire Worker*. It suggests that those contributing to these publications tended to assert the supremacy of class over race, whereas in Australia (and South Africa) the opposite was generally the case. Its conclusion is that 'The "white-settler" positions of Australia and South Africa within the British imperial network, combined with other national "peculiarities", largely accounted for their dominant socialist racism.'

So were Kirk's male, white activists comrades as well as cousins? His judgements are nicely nuanced: although labour activists in all three countries were interested in international links, they were influenced, he finds, primarily by national concerns and national interests, their internationalism and universalism undermined by sexism and racism. It is difficult, Kirk concedes, to draw lessons from the past. However, he believes that 'as reasoned by many British socialists a century ago, the essays in this study do lend themselves to the argument that labour in the twenty-first century has most to gain from a strategy of inclusiveness under conditions of capitalist globalization.'

Comrades and Cousins is a little disappointing. The three national case studies are informative, interesting and illuminating, but they do not gain a great deal by being placed alongside one another, and they do not contribute as much as one might wish to our understanding of globalisation and its discontents.

John Benson
University of Wolverhampton

Andrew Taylor, *The NUM and British Politics, Volume I: 1944–68* (Ashgate, Aldershot, 2003), ISBN 0-7546-0690-2, 269pp., £45.00 hbk.

This book is the first of two volumes on the National Union of Mineworkers (NUM) and British Politics. It represents a welcome addition to a mining historiography that is still largely concerned with the earlier period of private ownership and set-piece battles between capital and labour. The focus is institutional and the structure is chronological, beginning with the reorganisation of the Miners' Federation of Great Britain (MFGB) in 1944, and ending with the radicalisation of sections of the union in response to pit closures in 1968. Taylor claims throughout the text that the relationship between the NCB and the NUM was always an unequal one. The union was further weakened by its commitment to parliamentary politics as a strategy for pressing its claims.

The first chapter reaffirms the view that the union was not significantly altered by its metamorphosis into the NUM. The new Areas of the NUM were modelled on the old Districts of the MFGB retaining rulebooks, finances, and political traditions that reinforced the autonomy of individual coalfields. In the strongest section of the book, Taylor examines miners' response to nationalisation in 1947. The text here moves beyond the purely institutional by utilising the Mass Observation Archive. Oral testimony reinforces the view that in the early years there were criticisms of the scope and practice of public ownership. The chapter on the 1950s concentrates on the relationship between the NUM, the NCB and the government. The utilisation of party records offers welcome insights into conservative thinking on the future of coal. The Conservatives were reluctant to radically tinker with the coal industry and remained committed to ensuring the success of the industry.

According to Taylor, divisions within the union were maintained by the politics of the Cold War, whereby a right-wing majority was able to defend orthodox labour politics against more socialist critics. This is a rather simplistic view of the union in the 1950s. The National Executive Committee (NEC) of the union seemed to be divided by left-right factionalism, but the internal politics of the organisation was more complex. There was a left tradition in the union that was critical of communism. Epitomised by Tom Stephenson, the long-serving NEC representative of the Cumberland miners, and by branch officials like Lance Rogers in South Wales, its roots were in the Independent Labour Party. Similarly, on the right, coalfield moderates did not always act as a cohesive block. In the election for general secretary in 1959, Sam Watson and his Durham miners refused to endorse Sid Ford and supported the South Wales communist Bill Paynter. There were other members of the NEC, such as Ted Jones of the small North Wales Area, who saw themselves as pragmatists putting the welfare of the union above factional politics.

The final part of the book deals with the colliery closures and the subsequent tensions between the NUM and the Labour government after the general election victory in 1966. Taylor claims that this period 'demonstrated the relative powerlessness of the NUM in Labour's internal politics because of history, loyalty, and judgement that any Labour government was better than a Conservative government' (p.213). This is problematic. As the author himself claims, miners continued to vote Labour and were also reaping the benefits of high employment levels and improved working conditions. Memories of brutal coal owners, the struggle for union recognition and the pain of 1926 loomed large in the collective psyche. Yet to suggest that this was the only reason that miners stayed loyal to Labour is misleading. Many thought that the nationalised industry was a viable project that owed much to socialist planning. Sons of miners took advantage of the management training scheme and were committed to a system of industrial relations that worked to minimise disruption. Tom Ellis in North Wales and Ned Smith in Kent were colliery managers who were committed to working closely with the union and ensuring the long-term success of the industry. Communists such as Arthur Horner and Bill Paynter were close friends with the NCB chairman Jim Bowman through a shared background as miners and in trade union activism. Even the Tory-appointed Alf Robens, who replaced Bowman as chairman of the NCB in 1961, was a former trade union official who was popular across the coalfields. He would regularly share platforms with the NUM at Area galas and was comfortable speaking with miners on his visits underground. Contrary to the view promoted in the text the relationship was not a top-down one of miners' leaders slavishly following the diktats of experts and finding it 'impossible to envisage any political or industrial strategy other than those of nationalisation and parliamentary politics' (p.10). Area officials such as Sam Watson and Joe Gormley invested intellect, time, and energy into making nationalisation work and were pragmatic enough to realise that parliamentary politics was a strategy for delivering change. They supported the Labour leadership's 'interpretation of social democracy' (p.137), because it was one that many of them believed in.

The author confesses that this is a traditional study with an institutional focus concentrating on political processes. 'There is no consideration in this book of politics within coalfields or with the complexities of day-to-day pit politics' (p.viii). This is a major weakness. Because of its concentration on the national organisation the text is somewhat claustrophobic. The reader feels trapped within the national institution. There is no real sense of what a miner's life was like in the colliery, the mining community, the local lodge or indeed his own Area union. The individual voices that do appear from the national records are not complemented by any biographical background. To understand the politics of the individuals cited there needs to be a sense of the particular coalfield cultures from which they emerged.

A greater use of biography and autobiography would have given the narrative more life and a sense of drama. The quotations used are mostly from those sympathetic to the competing positions being taken at successive national conferences. Taylor stresses that 'the NUM was the creation of, and articulated, a particular view of what it was to be a mineworker' (p.viii). But to many miners the debates at national conference meant little to the everyday running of their particular pit. Their identity was reflected more in their Area organisations than it was in the national union. Moreover, economic and cultural change in the 1950s and 1960s led miners to see beyond the confines of the industry. Pit closures might have produced protest but many coalfields still had difficulty in recruiting youth.

The book represents a challenge to recent revisionist approaches to the history of the coal industry and seeks to defend the much-maligned view that miners represented the vanguard of British trade unionism. Taylor claims that 'mineworkers often saw themselves as amongst the most conscious and solidaristic section of the industrial working class...the emphasis on differentiation and fragmentation has obscured the efforts made to overcome these tendencies within the NUM' (p.vii). Taylor could have expanded this claim by engaging with the more recent literature that has emphasised 'differentiation' and 'fragmentation'. This can also be said of his handling of the impact of nationalisation. Following the line promoted by Vic Allen in an earlier study, the author claims that 'despite the veneer of socialist rhetoric and expectation the Morrisonian public corporation was a technocratic and conservative organisation compatible with and indeed essential to, the capitalist economy' (p.245). In line with other writers who have attacked nationalisation from the left Taylor provides no sense of how an alternative 'socialist' coal industry would have operated in the context of global capitalism, or indeed what a 'socialist' coal industry would have looked like. Contrary to what is claimed throughout the text, the Morrisonian public corporation was for the most part successful in resolving management-worker conflict, preventing a national dispute for twenty-five years.

The volume reads more like a work of political science rather than history and general readers might have difficulty in navigating their way through the minutiae of government policy and NCB-NUM relations. Nonetheless, *The NUM and British Politics* is a welcome addition to the still limited literature on the post-1944 British coal industry and we can look forward to the publication of the second volume. It will be interesting to see how the author handles the complexity of the 1984–5 dispute. It is hoped that the text will move beyond the tight institutional framework adopted in the first volume.

Keith Gildart
University of Wolverhampton

Bryan D. Palmer, *Cultures of Darkness: Night Travels in the Histories of Transgression* (Monthly Review Press, New York, 2000), ISBN 1-58367-027-0, viii-xiii + 609pp., $24.00, pbk.

Brian Palmer's fascinating book both heeds the postmodernist call for 'attention to marginality and identity' and provides a typically challenging critique of postmodernism's very assumptions, approach and epistemology. Palmer's focus rests upon 'illuminating moments of the experiences of class, race, and gender in particular historical periods of their formation'. This involves due attention to 'relations of dominance and subordination, rooted always in the social relations of production'. The author is not concerned with capitalism's mainstream or 'day-time' subjects, especially factory-based male workers, but with those on the 'night-time' periphery, often 'marginalized and despised' and inhabiting 'dark cultures distanced from the public visibilities of the day'. The aim is to explore their lives, their thoughts and actions, for dialectical instances of 'struggle and opposition, alternative and independence, complicity and incorporation, accommodation and escape'.

'Freed from certain conventions of the day, its shadows shielding the oppressed from the glare and gaze of power', the night, according to Palmer, 'could be the positive moment of alienation's transcendence, a space for self's realization in acts of rebellious alternative'. This was 'an environment of transgression', a 'time and place where power's constraints might be shed and powerlessness's aspirations articulated'. Yet night could also be associated less with 'liberation' than with 'estrangement and marginality', 'darkness within darkness, a discomforting anarchy of alienation and distress that shattered the brittle securities of daylight in fearful and terrifying dangers'. Palmer's aim is 'to touch down on some chapters' in this history of 'marginality and transgression', to 'place together' these 'selected and partial' chapters and, as such, 'to begin the process whereby an historical metanarrative of transgressive travel might be mapped'.

The book is a forceful and substantial example of Palmer's continuing 'Thompsonian'/materialist critique of, and direct challenge to, postmodernism. Palmer acknowledges the importance of studying discursive representations of self and 'otherness', of plurality, difference and fragmentation, *but* within an evolving social system or 'structure' of power and exploitation in which 'connexions' and 'commonalities' may be shown to exist. Against the postmodernist 'reification' of individual identity and choice and the 'anarchistic refusal of all metanarrative', the author calls for a non-reductionist re-connexion and exploration of 'the individual' and 'the social', structure, action and consciousness.

Palmer observes that while we 'cannot do...without a sober appreciation of the day's determinations', as highlighted by Marx, yet 'Marxist critique has nevertheless looked inadequately into the night and paid insufficient attention to dimensions of subordination, marginalization, and transgression not directly and unambiguously connected, via the wage and struggles over its contents, to the labor-capital relation'. While noting that 'that relation was central' to 'the evolution of other arenas of social contestation', Palmer explores some of these other, night-time, arenas. In so doing he both acknowledges his debt to Foucault's studies of marginalised others and relationships of power beyond the capitalist workplace and helps us to make connexions between capitalism's day-time and night-time subjects and experiences.

Palmer's exploration is both wide-ranging and impressive. In over 450 pages of text it addresses the experiences of peasants, witches, pirates and maroons, libertines, the 'dangerous classes', radicals and Jacobins, bandits and Mafiosi and the subject areas of 'Class and Gender in the Dissolution of the *Ancien Régime*', the 'Age of Revolution', 'Empire and Race', the 'underworlds' of the tavern, crime and protest, 'Eroticism and Revolutions' (including studies of 'Transgressive Sexualities' and 'The Fascist Night'), 'Blues, Jazz and Jookin' and 'Nights of Race Rage and Riot'. Set against the birth, development and maturation of transnational industrial capitalism, Palmer's studies are uniformly thought provoking and in many cases fascinating. Whether the book could have been written in a style and language more accessible to the non-specialist academic, and whether, in casting its net so wide, it fails fully to explore the *connexions* among its many and varied subjects and areas, will be matters for debate. (I would have welcomed an additional chapter building upon Palmer's important, but brief, comments concerning the substantive and methodological problems and benefits involved in exploring these connexions.) However, I enjoyed this book immensely. It is bold, ambitious and stimulating. Above all, perhaps, Palmer is to be congratulated upon constructively advancing rather than negatively freezing debate between materialists and postmodernists and in opening up new research areas and possible connexions in the history of capitalism's day-time and night-time.

Neville Kirk
Manchester Metropolitan University